FRANK
LLOYD
WRIGHT

THE CHELSEA HOUSE LIBRARY OF BIOGRAPHY

FRANK LLOYD WRIGHT

YONA ZELDIS McDONOUGH

Chelsea House Publishers

New York • Philadelphia

CHELSEA HOUSE PUBLISHERS

Editor-in-Chief   Remmel Nunn
Managing Editor   Karyn Gullen Browne
Copy Chief   Mark Rifkin
Picture Editor   Adrian Allen
Art Director   Maria Epes
Assistant Art Director   Noreen Romano
Manufacturing Manager   Gerald Levine
Systems Manager   Lindsey Ottman
Production Manager   Joseph Romano
Production Coordinator   Marie Claire Cebrián

The Chelsea House Library of Biography
Senior Editor   Kathy Kuhtz

Staff for FRANK LLOYD WRIGHT
Associate Editor   Scott Prentzas
Copy Editor   Christopher Duffy
Editorial Assistant   Tamar Levovitz
Picture Researcher   Pat Burns
Designer   Basia Niemczyc
Cover Illustration   Patti Oleon (from a photo by William Short)

3   5   7   9   8   6   4   2

Library of Congress Cataloging-in-Publication Data

McDonough, Yona Zeldis.
Frank Lloyd Wright/Yona Zeldis McDonough.
p. cm.—(The Chelsea House library of biography)
Includes bibliographical references and index.
Summary: Describes the life and career of the famous architect.
ISBN 0-7910-1626-9
    0-7910-1633-1 (pbk.)
1. Wright, Frank Lloyd, 1867–1959—Juvenile literature. 2. Architects—
United States—Biography—Juvenile literature. [1. Wright, Frank Lloyd,
1867–1959. 2. Architects.] I. Title. II. Series.
NA737.W7M37 1991   91-9278
720'.92—dc20   CIP
[B]   AC

Contents

THE CHELSEA HOUSE LIBRARY OF BIOGRAPHY

Other titles in the series are forthcoming.

Learning from Biographies

Vito Perrone

The oldest narratives that exist are biographical. Much of what we know, for example, about the Pharaohs of ancient Egypt, the builders of Babylon, the philosophers of Greece, the rulers of Rome, the many biblical and religious leaders who provide the base for contemporary spiritual beliefs, has come to us through biographies—the stories of their lives. Although an oral tradition was long the mainstay of historically important biographical accounts, the oral stories making up this tradition became by the 1st century A.D. central elements of a growing written literature.

In the 1st century A.D., biography assumed a more formal quality through the work of such writers as Plutarch, who left us more than 500 biographies of political and intellectual leaders of Rome and Greece. This tradition of focusing on great personages lasted well into the 20th century and is seen as an important means of understanding the history of various times and places. We learn much, for example, from Plutarch's writing about the collapse of the Greek city-states and about the struggles in Rome over the justice and the constitutionality of a world empire. We also gain considerable understanding of the definitions of morality and civic virtue and how various common men and women lived out their daily existence.

Not surprisingly, the earliest American writing, beginning in the 17th century, was heavily biographical. Those Europeans who came to America were dedicated to recording their experience, especially the struggles they faced in building what they determined to be a new culture. John Norton's *Life and Death of John Cotton*, printed in 1630, typifies these early works. Later biographers often tackled more ambitious projects. Cotton Mather's *Magnalia Christi Americana*, published in 1702, accounted for the lives of more than 70 ministers and political leaders. In addition, a biographical literature around the theme of Indian captivity had considerable popularity. Soon after the American Revolution and the organization of the United States of America, Americans were treated to a large outpouring of biographies about such figures as Benjamin Franklin, George Washington, Thomas Jefferson, and Aaron Burr, among others. These particular works served to build a strong sense of national identity.

Among the diverse forms of historical literature, biographies have been over many centuries the most popular. And in recent years interest in biography has grown even greater, as biography has gone beyond prominent government figures, military leaders, giants of business, industry, literature, and the arts. Today we are treated increasingly to biographies of more common people who have inspired others by their particular acts of courage, by their positions on important social and political issues, or by their dedicated lives as teachers, town physicians, mothers, and fathers. Through this broader biographical literature, much of which is featured in the CHELSEA HOUSE LIBRARY OF BIOGRAPHY, our historical understandings can be enriched greatly.

What makes biography so compelling? Most important, biography is a human story. In this regard, it makes of history something personal, a narrative with which we can make an intimate connection. Biographers typically ask us as readers to accompany them on a journey through the life of another person, to see some part of the world through another's eyes. We can, as a result, come to understand what it is like to live the life of a slave, a farmer, a textile worker, an engineer, a poet, a president—in a sense, to walk in another's shoes. Such experience can be personally invaluable. We cannot ask for a better entry into historical studies.

Although our personal lives are likely not as full as those we are reading about, there will be in most biographical accounts many common experiences. As with the principal character of any biography, we are also faced with numerous decisions, large and small. In the midst of living our lives we are not usually able to comprehend easily the significance of our daily decisions or grasp easily their many possible consequences, but we can gain important insights into them by seeing the decisions made by others play themselves out. We can learn from others.

Because biography is a personal story, it is almost always full of surprises. So often, the personal lives of individuals we come across historically are out of view, their public personas masking who they are. It is through biography that we gain access to their private lives, to the acts that define who they are and what they truly care about. We see their struggles within the possibilities and limitations of life, gaining insight into their beliefs, the ways they survived hardships, what motivated them, and what discouraged them. In the process we can come to understand better our own struggles.

As you read this biography, try to place yourself within the subject's world. See the events as that person sees them. Try to understand why the individual made particular decisions and not others. Ask yourself if you would have chosen differently. What are the values or beliefs that guide the subject's actions? How are those values or beliefs similar to yours? How are they different from yours? Above all, remember: You are engaging in an important historical inquiry as you read a biography, but you are also reading a literature that raises important personal questions for you to consider.

The Imperial Hotel—a vast, imposing structure made of brick, concrete, and sculptured lava—opened in 1922. Wright placed the hotel on a flexible foundation, which enabled it to survive the intense shocks of the 1923 earthquake.

1

Earthquake!

ON SEPTEMBER 1, 1923, Tetsuzo Inamaru, the assistant manager of Tokyo's newly built Imperial Hotel, had his hands full. A large, important party was scheduled to dine in the hotel's elegant Peacock Room, and Inamaru was busy ensuring that everything was arranged perfectly. The Imperial Hotel, designed and built by American architect Frank Lloyd Wright, had been plagued with financial and technical problems since its inception. Now that the hotel was completed, its owners were worried that the high construction costs—three times the original estimate of 3 million yen—would offset their anticipated profits.

The previous day, the staff had meticulously scrubbed and polished the hotel in preparation for the luncheon. The morning of September 1 was a hectic one for Inamaru, but he was finally able to take a break in his office before the guests were due to arrive. Before he could breathe easily, however, he felt the building quiver and immediately realized that an earthquake had struck. He hurried to the kitchen, where he was

Residents survey the damage caused by a powerful earthquake that struck Tokyo, Japan, on September 1, 1923. Most of the city's buildings were destroyed by the quake and the ensuing fires.

confronted by the terrifying sight of boiling fat leaping out of pans and exploding on the electric ranges. Fearing a massive fire, he ordered that all power in the hotel be cut off immediately.

He then ran to the Peacock Room. As he entered the chamber, another forceful tremor shook the building. The beautiful chairs, plates, and silverware—all designed by Wright—shuddered as the floor rocked beneath them. But miraculously, the walls and ceilings did not cave in. Only the electric fans on the balconies fell, dropping to the floor at Inamaru's feet in a series of dull thuds. Buildings throughout Tokyo crumbled and collapsed, but the Imperial Hotel remained standing.

A few days later, a telegram arrived at Frank Lloyd Wright's studio in Spring Green, Wisconsin. It read: "Hotel Stands Undamaged as Monument of Your Genius. Hundreds of Homeless Provided by Perfectly Maintained Service. Congratulations." The telegram was signed by Baron Okura, chairman of the board of directors of the corporation that had financed the construction of the hotel. Newspapers later published the contents of the telegram, which gave the false impression that the Imperial Hotel was the only building to emerge unscathed from the earthquake. Wright biographer Brendan Gill has also pointed out that the telegram was datelined Spring Green, not Tokyo, thus raising the suspicion that Wright sent it himself.

Although the Imperial Hotel was not the only building to survive the quake, it did weather the disaster virtually intact. Wright's design contributed to that feat, and he became widely known as an architect who outsmarted a terrible natural disaster. Certainly the possibility of earthquake was in the forefront of his mind when he designed the hotel. Wright describes his approach to the problem in *An Autobiography* (1933):

> The terror of the temblor [earthquake] never left me while
> I planned the building nor while, for more than four years,

I worked upon it. . . . I studied the temblor. Found it a wave-movement, not of sea but earth—accompanied by a shock no rigidity could withstand. . . . Because of the wave movements, deep foundations like long piles would oscillate and rock the structure. Therefore the foundation should be short or shallow. There was sixty to seventy feet of soft mud below the upper depth of eight feet of surface soil on the site. That mud seemed a merciful provision—a good cushion to relieve the terrible shocks. Why not float the building upon it? A battleship floats on salt water. . . . Why not, then, a building made as the two hands thrust together palms inward, fingers interlocking and yielding to movement—but resilient to return to original position when distortion ceased? . . . Why fight the quake? Why not sympathize with it and outwit it?

The durability of the Imperial Hotel and the publicity surrounding its creator demonstrate two key elements in Wright's life and art: his lifelong insistence on working with, rather than against, nature and his tendency to mythologize himself.

Throughout his life, Wright zealously advocated the adoption of what he called organic architecture, insisting that architects harmonize their buildings with nature and with the needs of the inhabitants. Ever mindful of the features of building materials and the landscape, Wright conceived the Imperial Hotel in harmony with, rather than opposed to, the natural forces with which it would have to contend.

Wright was also prone to embellish aspects of his life for dramatic and promotional purposes, often without regard for accuracy. Some people found this trait annoying and, on certain occasions, accused Wright of being a liar. Others have accepted this trait as simply another facet of his complicated and legendary genius. Whatever the interpretation, one thing remains certain: The prodigious work and colorful life of this unusual self-made man remain compelling long after his death.

The striking shapes of the Imperial Hotel's dining room reflect Wright's passionate concern with the meaningful configuration of interior space. He once wrote that "architecture [should be] spiritually conceived as the appropriate enclosure of interior space. . . . The enclosed space . . . is the reality of the building."

Frank, age three, sports a fashionable outfit in this 1870 photograph. Four years later, his family moved from Richland Center, Wisconsin, to Weymouth, Massachusetts.

2

Boyhood: Weymouth and Spring Green

IN 1876, WILLIAM WRIGHT, a Baptist minister, and his wife, Anna Lloyd-Jones Wright, traveled by train from Boston to Philadelphia to view the marvels of the heralded Centennial Exposition. While strolling through the many fascinating pavilions, Anna Wright chanced upon an exhibit of unusual toys that caught her attention. The simple, streamlined blocks—cut from smooth, handsome wood into geometric shapes and painted in vivid primary colors—seemed to her a welcome relief from the gaudy excesses typical of toys in the Victorian period. The woman in charge of the display had been trained in Austria by the blocks' inventor, Friedrich Froebel (a German educator who founded the kindergarten system), and she explained the educational theories that lay behind the blocks. Delighted with the whole concept, Anna, a teacher herself, purchased a set for her nine-year-old son, Frank.

Years later, Frank Lloyd Wright described the joy that he found in those simple toys and how they influenced his entire architectural perspective: "The smooth shapely maple blocks with which to build, the sense of which never afterward leaves the fingers. . . . The early . . . experiencè with the straight line, the flat plane; the square; the triangle; the circle! . . . These primary forms and figures were the secret of all effects . . . which were ever got into the world of architecture."

Surveying the more than 700 buildings that Wright designed during his long, productive career, one is easily convinced of the accuracy of this recollection. His love for pure, clean forms that evoke geometric clarity is evident from his earliest works to his latest. From the emphatic, sprawling rectangular shapes of the midwestern prairie houses to the multitiered cone of the Solomon R. Guggenheim Museum in New York City, Wright always remained true to the unadorned simplicity that he learned while handling the Froebel blocks.

Yet as instrumental as the blocks were on his future vision, they represented only a single step in a course that Anna had been plotting for years. So certain that the child she carried would be a great architect, she hung engravings of English cathedrals on the walls of the nursery even before his birth. Throughout Frank's early years, Anna was a powerful influence, and her uncomplicated, yet highly refined, taste was something that he grew to appreciate and share.

Anna had a compelling heritage of her own. Daughter of a sturdy Welsh clan of ministers, educators, and farmers who had settled in the rolling hills of southern Wisconsin, she was a teacher when she met her future husband, William Wright. Her father, the pioneer Richard Jones, had been trained as a hatter and was an outspoken Unitarian. Unitarianism—a Christian denomination whose adherents believe that God exists in one being, support individual freedom of belief, and stress faith in the universal brotherhood of humankind—was decidedly unpopular in Wales. But Jones had energy and charisma enough to attract Mary Lloyd, a gentle young woman from a well-to-do Welsh family. She had to brave strong public censure when she married so far beneath her social station. The young couple, who now called themselves Lloyd-Jones, moved with their seven children from Wales to southern Wisconsin in 1845. There they established an enclave near the village of Spring Green, not far from Madison, the state capital. The Lloyd-Jones children flourished in their new home. Anna's brother Jenkin became a well-known Unitarian minister; her two sisters, Ellen and Jane, were also teachers and eventually founded a boarding school for adolescents on the family land.

Anna was 29 years old when she married William Russell Cary Wright on August 17, 1866. Wright was 46 years old and already had 3 children by his previous marriage. Some evidence suggests that he was born in England and immigrated with his family to the United States while still an

These educational toys, known as Froebel blocks, profoundly influenced Wright's architectural perspective. As a child, he played with these simple geometric shapes, learning many of the basic principles of building and design.

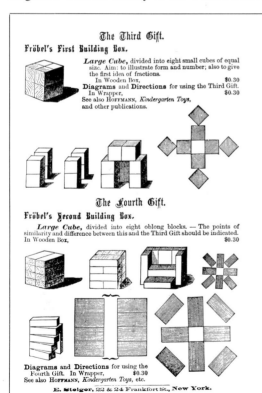

The Third Gift.

Fröbel's First Building Box.

Large Cube, divided into eight small cubes of equal size. Aim: to illustrate form and number; also to give the first idea of fractions.
In Wooden Box, $0.30
Diagrams and **Directions** for using the Third Gift. In Wrapper, $0.30
See also Hoffmann, *Kindergarten Toys,* and other publications.

The Fourth Gift.

Fröbel's Second Building Box.

Large Cube, divided into eight oblong blocks. — The points of similarity and difference between this and the Third Gift should be indicated.
In Wooden Box, $0.30

Diagrams and **Directions** for using the Fourth Gift. In Wrapper, $0.30
See also Hoffmann, *Kindergarten Toys,* etc.

E. Steiger, 22 & 24 Frankfort St., New York.

The Fifth Gift.

Fröbel's Third Building Box.

This is a continuation of, and complement to, the Third Gift. It consists of twenty-one *whole,* six *half-,* and twelve *quarter-*cubes, forming altogether *one large Cube.*

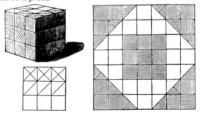

In Wooden Box, $0.75
Diagrams and **Directions** for using the Fifth Gift. In Wrapper, $0.60
See also Hoffmann, *Kindergarten Toys,* etc.

The Fifth Gift B.

The Fifth Building Box (a combination of the Fifth and Second Gifts). In Wooden Box, $1.00
Diagrams and **Directions** for using the Fifth Gift **B.** In Wrapper, $0.50

The Sixth Gift.

Fröbel's Fourth Building Box.

This is a continuation of, and complement to, the Fourth Gift. It consists of eighteen *whole* oblong blocks, three similar blocks divided lengthwise, and six divided breadthwise, forming altogether *one large Cube.*
In Wooden Box, $0.75
Diagrams and **Directions** for using the Sixth Gift. In Wrapper, $0.60
See also Hoffmann, *Kindergarten Toys,* etc.

The Fifth Gift (Froebel's Third Building Box), *extra-large size,* 1½ cubic feet. In strong Wooden Box, $7.20
The Sixth Gift (Froebel's Fourth Building Box), *extra-large size,* 1½ cubic feet. In strong Wooden Box, $9.00

E. Steiger, 22 & 24 Frankfort St., New York.

infant. William's father was a Baptist minister in Hartford, Connecticut, for many years. William attended Amherst College and prepared for a degree in law. But the moody, artistic, and somewhat eccentric young man had no aptitude for a legal career and abandoned the idea early on.

Anna Wright was so convinced that Frank would be a great architect that she hung engravings of English cathedrals on the walls of the nursery even before he was born. As Frank grew older, he began to appreciate and share his mother's uncomplicated, yet highly refined, decorative tastes.

After he graduated from college, William eked out a living as an itinerant music teacher; music was the only field for which he felt any real passion. His travels led him to the Wisconsin River valley, where he met and married Permelia Holcomb. They had three children, but when his wife died in 1864, Wright in effect abandoned the children and resumed his wandering life.

While presiding over a singing bee (a community social gathering at which songs are sung) near Spring Green, Wright met Anna Lloyd-Jones. Despite the difference in their ages and his lack of financial success, she was utterly taken with what she felt to be Wright's spiritual aspirations and with the music of his soul. Soon after they married, William revealed to Anna that he had decided to become a minister. This only confirmed Anna's choice, for the current of religious feeling in the Lloyd-Jones clan ran strong and deep.

Their first child, Frank Lloyd Wright, was born in Richland Center, Wisconsin, on June 8, 1867. Seven years later, William moved his family to Weymouth, Massachusetts, where he became the minister of a small Baptist church. His salary did not provide much in the way of luxuries for the family, but the parishioners were kind, and Frank, wearing the long curls that were fashionable at the time, was generously allowed to attend a private school at no charge.

Humble living did not, however, prevent Anna from exhibiting her tasteful sense of interior decoration at the manse. Etchings on clean white mats; spotless net curtains; Oriental rugs; maple and rattan furniture; dried leaves arranged in simple glass vases so that the stems could be seen—these were the things with which she liked to surround herself and her family. Years later, when Wright wrote down his own ideas about interior design, they corresponded in many significant details to the environment that his mother had carefully constructed during his childhood.

William Wright was an emotionally remote and distant parent, but he displayed a fanatic concern with his son's musical education. Frank claimed that his father taught him the structural similarities between music and buildings.

Frank's parents fostered his artistic development by encouraging him to pursue creative hobbies. As a boy, he kept a collection of stones chosen for their unusual shapes. He also spent a great deal of time drawing with colored pencils; throughout Frank's life, the sight of such pencils filled him with a great sense of inner peace and satisfaction.

Although Anna was undoubtedly a guiding influence on her son's later artistic life, William also contributed to his son's aesthetic development. An emotionally remote and distant father, he nonetheless displayed a fanatical concern with Frank's musical education. At the age of seven, the boy could play Bach compositions on the piano. William installed a valuable pipe organ in the Weymouth church, and Frank later recalled how he once pumped the organ by hand for his demanding parent until he lay exhausted on the floor, unable to continue pumping.

Whatever else the Wrights may have lacked in material comfort, there was always music. Listening to the concertos of Beethoven, which would sometimes fill the house far into the night, Frank would lie awake and imagine "an edifice of sound." Wright always claimed that it was his father who taught him the structural similarities between buildings and music.

The family remained in New England until about 1877, when they returned to Wisconsin, this time to Madison, where Frank continued his education at the Second Ward School. The Wrights established residence in an undistinguished house on Gorham Street. Yet the interior remained a visual oasis—a testimony to Anna's enduring sense of taste and design. And by 1880, the household boasted three children—Frank and his two younger sisters, Jane and Maginel.

Despite the presence of the University of Wisconsin, Madison was at the time a scattered, untidy midwestern settlement with few refinements to satisfy Frank's increasing appetite for visual and intellectual stimulation. He was a voracious reader as a child, and whenever he found life on Gorham Street a bit dull, there were plenty of books around to divert him. Once, his aunts Nell and Jane gave him a copy of John Ruskin's *Seven Lamps of Architecture* (1849). Ruskin, an influential English essayist and critic, wrote extensively on architecture. All the family members had been made aware of Frank's future destiny—for true to his mother's wishes, becoming an architect was his dream.

Frank could escape the drudgery of Madison during the vacations spent at the Lloyd-Jones farm at Spring Green.

Every summer, Uncle James Lloyd-Jones came for the three Wright children in a creaky old wagon drawn by a massive team of horses. At first, Frank found farm work difficult, tedious, and, at times, disgusting. In *An Autobiography*, he cataloged the things that he least liked: the daily routine of being roused at four in the morning to do the milking; the

jobs of chopping off the heads of roosters and slitting the throats of hogs; and the time he contracted lice from the hens. On one occasion, he actually ran away from the farm and was found at the ferry across the Wisconsin River. There was no punishment for his desertion, only the gentle but firm insistence of his uncle that he continue to do his chores.

Wright (seated to the right of the empty chair), age 16, joins the Lloyd-Jones clan for this 1883 family portrait. Wright spent many summers during his youth at the Lloyd-Jones's farm in Spring Green, Wisconsin.

But gradually, Frank's sense of mastery over his assigned tasks grew, and he came to love the rolling black hills that had nurtured and sustained his mother's people. He appreciated the many beauties, as well as the hardships, of a life regulated by the seasons' natural rhythms. He found that even the farm machinery—such as the bright red combine with its reels of yellow, blue, and green—was visually appealing.

For about five years, the family spent summers at the farm and winters in Madison. During these years, the domestic problems of Frank's parents grew steadily worse. Depressed, bored, tired, and profoundly disappointed, William decided that his home life was unbearable. Anna, too, was miserable and took an unusual step for a woman of her era when she told him, "Well, Mr. Wright, leave us. I will manage with the children. Go your way." William took her at her word; he packed a few of his things, tucked his violin under his arm, and left the family for good. Neither Anna nor the children ever saw him again.

Once William had gone, Frank found himself, at the age of 18, the man of the family. He realized that he was obligated to help support his mother and sisters and wondered how he would acquire the education necessary to become an architect—for that was still his dream. He thought the best way of achieving his grand ambitions would be to set off for the glittering promise held by Chicago, which was only 139 miles south of Madison. But his mother wanted him to stay at home, and his stern uncle Jenkin Lloyd-Jones agreed: "On no account should the young man come to Chicago. He should stay in Madison and finish his education. That will do more for him than anything. If he came . . . he would only waste himself on fine clothes and girls." His mother offered this letter from her brother as proof that Frank belonged at home with her.

The letter angered Wright, but in deference to his uncle's advice, he took a job in the office of Allen D. Conover, a local builder. Because Wright actually knew nothing of practical value about his chosen career, Conover put him to work as an office boy and junior apprentice. Although Conover was more of an engineer than an architect, he received commissions for some of the most important buildings in Madison, including the university armory. From him,

English writer and critic John Ruskin (1819–1900) wrote several perceptive and influential treatises on architecture. Wright avidly read Ruskin's Seven Lamps of Architecture *(1849), which became an important influence on his development as an architect.*

Wright learned to value sound engineering over pure design. He never forgot the day that the new north wing of the Old Capitol came crashing down. Afterward, investigators discovered that dishonest contractors had fatally weakened the building by filling the piers (structural supports) with loose rubble.

While at Conover's, Wright worked hard, applying himself to learning every aspect of the engineering and drafting trades. He later recounted that one of his typical days involved installing the metal clips on the roof trusses of the university's Science Hall during its construction. Conover was, in Wright's estimation, "a cultivated and kindly man." He allowed his young assistant to follow a flexible schedule so that Wright could attend the University of Wisconsin as a special part-time student.

Architecture as a discipline was not taught at the university, so Wright had to make do with courses in drafting, taught by the Department of Civil Engineering, and descriptive geometry. An indifferent student, Wright did not excel in his studies and completed no more than three terms, a fact that he later tried to obscure. Instead of being proud of how much he had accomplished on his own, Wright felt throughout his life that his lack of formal training was a cause for shame and deception.

Although Anna was forced to return to teaching to help support the family (Frank's slender income from Conover not being sufficient), she still wanted him to have some of the pleasures that college offered. When the Phi Delta Theta fraternity tapped Wright for membership, she took her Swiss gold watch to a local pawnbroker to get him the money for the initiation fees. She also managed to buy a mink collar, which she sewed onto the overcoat that he wore to his first college prom.

Mink collar notwithstanding, the evening of the prom did not go smoothly. Young women made Wright very shy and nervous, and his date, May White—the pretty cousin of a

sophisticated classmate named Charlie Ware—was no ex-
ception. At the hall, he managed to lose her in the crowd,
and several dances went by before he found her again. Ware
smoothed things over as best he could by making sure his
cousin's dance program was filled, something that Wright
had neglected to do. At the end of the evening, when he
deposited her at her doorstep, he suddenly realized that he
was supposed to kiss her good night. So alarming was the
thought that he mumbled something about having had a
good time and rushed back to his carriage without making
sure that she was safely inside the dormitory. During his
sophomore year, Wright gamely attended the annual dance
again, this time escorting Blanche Ryder, a tactful young
woman from town. The evening went somewhat better than
the first one.

Despite Anna's efforts to give her son the sort of aca-
demic and social life she thought he deserved, Frank grew
bored and restless in Madison. His thoughts and dreams lay
elsewhere, and the prospect of Chicago continued to tanta-
lize him. He explained to his mother that there were great
buildings and great architects in Chicago, pleading that his
own future as an architect was utterly dependent on reaching
this magical city. Occasionally, Wright would lose his tem-
per, and a full-scale fight would ensue. Later, sorry for
hurting her, he would calm down for a while.

But one day, after brooding alone in his room, where the
prints of English cathedrals still hung, Wright went down-
stairs to the study. His father's books were still on the
shelves. He took down the calf-bound volumes by the ancient Greek biographer Plutarch and a set of books by the
English historian Edward Gibbon. To these he added the
mink collar from his coat and paid a visit to the local
pawnbroker, who advanced him seven dollars on the lot.
With this money, Wright went straight to the station and
boarded the very next train for Chicago without going home
to say good-bye.

Wright posed for this portrait in 1889, two years after arriving in Chicago. After working for slightly more than a year as a draftsman for architect Joseph Silsbee, Wright landed a job at Adler & Sullivan, one of the city's most prominent architectural firms.

3

Chicago: The City of Wonders

EMERGING FROM THE OLD WELLS DEPOT on a rainy spring evening in 1887, Wright had cause to doubt his impulsive flight from home. The noisy, crowded, gaslit streets of Chicago seemed unfriendly and ugly; he had only a few dollars and nowhere to stay. But after finding a room in a cheap hotel and deciding to restrict his food intake to doughnuts and coffee, he resolved to spend the next day looking for work in an architect's office.

In *An Autobiography*, Wright recalls trudging through the streets of the unfamiliar city for three days in a futile search for employment. On the fourth day, he began the morning without any breakfast and with just a few coins in his pocket. If he failed to find work, he faced the prospect of returning to Madison in defeat. But luck seemed to be with Wright when he walked into the office of architect Joseph Lyman Silsbee, where he was interviewed by Cecil Corwin, a young draftsman. Before he even looked at Wright's drawings, Corwin asked him if he were a minister's son. Wright was surprised and asked how he had guessed. Corwin replied that he too was the son of a clergyman and could always pick out another.

Corwin seemed pleased with Wright's drawings and asked him to wait. He was gone for a few minutes and then returned with Joseph Lyman Silsbee, one of Chicago's most successful residential architects. Silsbee—a tall, distinguished-looking man who wore his gold-rimmed eyeglasses suspended on a long gold chain around his neck—looked at Wright and said, "Take him on as a tracer—eight dollars." With those words, Frank Lloyd Wright landed his first job in Chicago.

But what Wright failed to recount, and what later biographers have noted, was that Silsbee already knew Wright's family because he had been commissioned to design the Unitarian All Souls Church in Chicago by none other than Wright's uncle Jenkin Lloyd-Jones. Sometime after this, in 1886, Silsbee produced a plan for Jones's Unity Chapel at Helena, Wisconsin. William C. Gannett, a well-known Unitarian minister, said that the interior of the church had been "looked after" by a "boy architect belonging to the family." Whether this meant that Wright designed the three interior rooms or supervised the building is unclear, but certainly he knew—and worked for—Silsbee before he ever reached Chicago. Further proof of this is suggested by the fact that when the rendering for the chapel was published, it bore Wright's own signature. And early in 1887, Wright designed a small Unitarian church for a congregation in Sioux City, Iowa, possibly with the help of Uncle Jenkin as well as Silsbee. Yet Wright always maintained that it was the strength of his drawings alone that got him the job in Silsbee's firm.

Although he was glad to have found work, Wright felt disappointed with the salary; he had hoped to be earning at least three times as much. Corwin must have sensed this. When Wright turned to leave, he invited the young man to be his guest for lunch at Kinsley's, a Chicago restaurant known for its corned beef hash. He then extended his

A row of buildings over-looks a crowded Chicago street in the early 1890s. Following the devastating fire of 1871, Chicago began an unprecedented rebuilding program. Its celebrated new buildings and great architects had lured Wright to the city to fulfill his dream of becoming an architect.

generosity even further by asking Wright to stay with his family until he found some decent lodgings. Wright gladly abandoned the dreary hotel for the clean, comfortable guest room at the Corwins'.

On his first night there, he asked Corwin for a pen and some paper, saying that he wanted to write to his mother. He also asked for a loan of $10, which he promised to pay back at a rate of $2 a week. Corwin gave Wright the stationery and the money. A few minutes later, he was standing in front of the corner mailbox, in which he dropped the envelope containing the very first money that he sent home.

With a job and a decent place to stay, Wright could enjoy some of the spectacles that Chicago offered. He saw his first electric light, traveled on a cable car for the first time, and attended his first ballet performance at the Chicago Opera House for the whopping price of one dollar. (Wright later boasted that he was always quick to spend money on luxuries because he knew that the necessities would eventually take care of themselves.)

Although Wright claimed that he was happy working for Silsbee, he still thought that his salary was insufficient. He had received a four-dollar raise, but that was offset when he moved to a furnished room on Vincennes Avenue. Things got so bad that when Silsbee refused to increase his salary to $15 a week, Wright left and took a job with the architect W. W. Clay. But with uncharacteristic humility, Wright later recalled that the work was totally beyond him and that he returned to Silsbee's office. Instead of

Soon after arriving in Chicago in 1887, Wright was captured in this photograph with his friend Cecil Corwin (right). Corwin, a draftsman in Silsbee's office, helped the callow 20-year-old adjust to life in the big city.

reprimanding him, Silsbee just peered over his gold-rimmed spectacles and said, "Ah Wright. Here you are again, eh? You may have eighteen dollars."

Although Wright spent barely a year in Silsbee's office, it proved to be an excellent training ground for his talents. From Silsbee he gained the respect for residential architecture that would be so important in his future career. Silsbee also allowed him plenty of room to grow and develop as an architect. While still an apprentice, Wright published three renderings (illustrations) under his own name. One, a combination school and house for his aunts Jane and Ellen Lloyd-Jones at Hillside, Wisconsin, was actually erected, chiefly because Silsbee permitted him time off to supervise the construction.

Despite Silsbee's many kindnesses and his own undeniable progress under Silsbee's supervision, Wright was restless. Working for Silsbee did not satisfy the young architect; he wanted something more. In his search for architectural mentors, he discovered the writings of Eugène-Emmanuel Viollet-le-Duc, the French architect and critic who had restored the cathedrals of Notre Dame and Sainte Chapelle in Paris, among others. Viollet-le-Duc endorsed "rational architecture," his notion that beauty in architecture depended on its conformance to function. He stressed that a building should always express its purpose. Wright was also influenced by *The Grammar of Ornament*, a book he found in the library of the All Souls Church. The author, English architect Owen Jones, declared five general propositions with which Wright agreed completely:

> The Decorative Arts rise from, and should be properly attendant upon, Architecture.

> Architecture is the material of the wants, the facilities, and the sentiments of the age in which it is created. Style in Architecture is the peculiar form that expression takes under the influence of climate and materials, at command.

As Architecture, so all works of Decorative Arts, should possess fitness, proportion, harmony, the result of all [of] which is repose.

True beauty results from that repose which the mind feels when eye, the intellect, and the affections are satisfied from any want.

Construction should never be decorated. Decoration should never be purposely constructed. That which is beautiful is true; that which is true must be beautiful.

But the most significant influence on Wright's philosophy of architecture was surely that of Louis Henri Sullivan, a Chicago architect whose buildings were acclaimed for their functional form, striking ornamentation, and signficance in the evolution of the skyscraper. Wright admired the older architect, and when he heard that Sullivan was looking for a draftsman with fine taste and good skills to help complete the drawings for a huge business block, hotel, and opera house for Congress Street and Michigan Avenue, Wright immediately applied for the position.

Sullivan, a small, excitable man with large brown eyes, interviewed the eager applicant. He looked over Wright's drawings carefully, some of which showed the influence of his own flowing, ornamental style. He then asked what Wright had been receiving in the way of salary. Wright declined to state the figure, saying only that it was not enough. "How much is enough?" Sullivan wanted to know. "Twenty-five dollars," replied Wright. Sullivan asked Wright to report to work on the following Monday.

When Silsbee learned of this, he expressed his disappointment to Wright. Although he felt a momentary pang at leaving his first employer in Chicago, Wright threw himself into his work with Sullivan and his partner, Dankmar Adler, a master engineer and the business-acquiring member of the firm. From the very start, Wright shone brightly in his new position. After a trial period, he received a raise and a private office just outside Sullivan's workroom. Although Sullivan was known for his rude and often contemptuous treatment of his employees, he was courteous and respectful to Wright. Wright in turn called Sullivan *Lieber Meister* (beloved master) and tried very hard to please him.

Sullivan's open favoritism toward Wright made the other draftsmen at Adler & Sullivan envious. Late one afternoon when the bosses were gone, the leader of the office bullies threw Wright's hat down the stairs. Acting swiftly, Wright punched the man, breaking his glasses and knocking him off his stool. The bully jumped up screaming and grabbed a knife used for sharpening pencils. He managed to inflict several cuts before Wright knocked him unconscious with a T square, one of the tools drafters use for making parallel lines. Wright was bleeding badly, and one of the other drafters hurried him to a doctor. Although Adler and Sullivan later heard about the incident, they said nothing about it, and there were no more fights. Sullivan did not care what happened to a common drafter as long as Wright, whom he called "the good pencil in his hand," was unharmed.

During this time, Wright's social life was mostly supervised by his uncle Jenkin, who lived in Chicago and was the pastor of the All Souls Church. Through his constant participation in parish parties, concerts, and amateur plays, Wright gradually overcame his shyness with girls. In one play, a stage adaptation of Victor-Marie Hugo's novel *Les Misérables*, he portrayed a French officer, wearing a sword, cavalry boots, and red coat. During the dance that followed the performance, Wright bumped into a pretty girl with such force that they both fell down. When he helped her up, he noticed just how pretty she was—blue eyes, very pink cheeks, and curly red-brown hair. Wright learned that she was Catherine Tobin, a 17-year-old student at Hyde Park High School, and he soon found someone to introduce them formally.

Louis Sullivan, an innovative designer, summarized his philosophy of architecture in his famous maxim Form follows function. *Sullivan, whom Wright called* Lieber Meister *(beloved master), had the greatest influence on Wright's architectural theories.*

Once introduced, the romance between them blossomed quickly. Frank escorted Catherine on walks and picnics, took her to parties and concerts, and lectured to her on his lofty ideas about life and art. Unfortunately for the young couple, everyone disapproved of the match—her parents, Wright's mother, and even his friend Cecil Corwin, who discouraged him from committing himself to the only girl whom he had ever kissed.

But Frank failed to be deterred from his aim, even when Catherine's parents tried to separate them by sending her away to Mackinac Island, Michigan, for three months. Wright turned to his mentor and friend, Louis Sullivan, telling him that he needed financial help. Sullivan responded by offering him a five-year contract. Once having obtained the security of a contract that now made him the highest-paid drafter in Chicago, Wright asked for yet another favor—$5,000 with which to buy a plot of land and build a house. In *An Autobiography*, Wright records their conversation:

> "Mr. Sullivan, if you want me to work for you as long as five years, couldn't you lend me enough money to build a little house and let me pay you back so much each month—taken out of my pay envelope?"

> Mr. Sullivan—it seemed—had a good deal of money of his own at the time. He took me to his lawyer. . . . The contract was signed, and then the Master went with me— "the pencil in his hand"—to see the lot I knew I wanted. It was Mr. Austin's gardener's, the plain lot, the lovely old tanglewood . . . The Master approved the lot and bought it. There was $3500 left over to build a small home on that ground planted by the old Scottish landscape gardener.

> "Now look out, Wright!" said Mr. Sullivan, "I know your tastes . . . no 'extras.'"

> I agreed. "No, none."

> But there was $1200 more to be paid toward the end. I kept this dark, paid it in due course as best I could out of what remained of my salary.

On June 1, 1889, Frank Lloyd Wright and Catherine Tobin were married on a rainy day, amid the gloomy predictions of their relatives. The mother of the groom fainted. The father of the bride wept, along with the minister performing the service, Wright's uncle Jenkin. Afterward, the newlyweds spent their honeymoon in Wisconsin with Wright's maternal relatives. A few weeks later, they returned by train to Oak Park, a suburb of Chicago, where Wright diligently began building a cozy cottage for his bride.

Frank's drawing of Catherine, his first wife, reveals her beauty and his considerable artistic abilities.

The Robie house (1909)—with its heavy brick masses, wide cantilevered balconies, low-hipped roofs, and striking horizontal planes—displays many of the features found in Wright's early residential designs. Many architectural historians believe that the Robie house is the most stunning example of his Prairie Style.

4

Going Solo: Oak Park and the Prairie Style

THE EARLY YEARS OF WRIGHT'S MARRIAGE seemed filled with promise. He had a beautiful, practical, and socially poised wife, a good job, a lovely home that he had built himself, and excellent prospects.

Wright's first house gave him a sense of enormous pride. Catherine later remarked that he never stopped tinkering with it from the moment they moved in. The Wrights' first Oak Park cottage was a simple six-room cube covered in brown cedar shingles with a high, pointed gable and casement windows. The living room featured a large open fireplace and an inglenook (a bench occupying the nook beside the fireplace), an architectural element that was very popular in England at the time and that Wright himself loved and used in many of his designs. To many people, the house looked like a seaside cottage, its style derived from houses on the chic East Coast.

With the birth of the Wrights' children—Frank Lloyd Wright, Jr. (called Lloyd), John, Catherine, David, Frances, and Llewellyn—their house grew and evolved to accommodate their various needs. Wright built them a beautiful playroom that had a mural from the *Arabian Nights* over its fireplace and was filled with dozens of games and toys that he made himself. He also built a separate studio for himself. A long corridor connected the studio with the house, and a willow tree grew through the corridor's roof. Everyone in Oak Park knew the Wrights' place as the "house with the tree growing through it." He also remodeled a small Gothic-style frame house that was already on the property for use by his mother and sisters, whom he had brought to Chicago in 1890.

As the family grew, so did Wright's concern with improving his earning power. He wanted to be able to provide

In 1890, Wright (front row, right) and his extended family sit outside their home in Oak Park, a suburb of Chicago. Wright found many clients among his Oak Park neighbors, which enabled him to build many impressive houses throughout the Chicago area.

himself, his wife, and his children with beautiful things of the finest quality—rugs, furniture, prints, and the like. Wright was not primarily interested in the status that such objects suggested; instead, he was deeply concerned about the pure aesthetic qualities that they possessed.

To supplement his salary at Adler & Sullivan, Wright began taking on a number of private assignments on his own. One of the most important of these was the house he designed and built for James Charnley, a wealthy Chicago lumberman. The Charnley house was to stand on Astor Street, a new thoroughfare that ran from Division Street to North Avenue. These six blocks were to become the site of some of Chicago's finest and most noteworthy homes.

Wright knew that his work would be on display, and he very much wanted it to stand out. Luckily, Charnley wanted something new and different in the way of design, and he commissioned Wright to create it.

The Charnley house, built in 1891, is a balanced structure in Roman brick on a stone base with crisp outlines that suggest the contours of the wooden Froebel blocks from Wright's childhood. The overall effect—created in part by the strong horizontal emphasis of the facade (the front or any side of a building that receives special architectural treatment) and the broad, flat planes it created—is stark, simple, and bold. Nothing like it had been seen before in Chicago, and Charnley was delighted.

The success of the Charnley house enabled Wright to obtain more private commissions. Between 1891 and 1893, he designed approximately 10 houses without the

In 1891, Wright—without the knowledge of Louis Sullivan—designed and built this simple, yet unconventional, house for James Charnley, a wealthy lumberman. The success of the Charnley house enabled Wright to obtain other private commissions.

knowledge of Louis Sullivan. Because Adler & Sullivan was too busy to take on smaller residential jobs, Wright felt there was no conflict of interest in accepting these commissions. But Sullivan saw things differently, as is clear from this passage in *An Autobiography*:

> Although I had not realized this, I had broken my contract by doing this outside work. So I protested. I asked the Master if I had been any less serviceable in the office lately.

> "No," he said, "but your sole interest is here, while your contract lasts. I won't tolerate division under any circumstances."

> This seemed unjust to me. If I could work over-hours at home for Adler & Sullivan and keep up my work in the office what harm in doing likewise for myself to relieve my own necessities? All the same I was wrong—I saw it but angered now by what seemed the injustice of the Master—it was the first time he had said harsh words to me—I appealed to Dankmar Adler.

> Mr. Adler interceded, which more deeply offended the Master than ever. . . . I threw my pencil down and walked out of the Adler & Sullivan office never to return. . . . Not for more than twelve years did I see Louis Sullivan again or communicate with him in any way.

The Willets house (1902), located in Highland Park (a Chicago suburb), was one of Wright's most significant prairie houses. Wright emphasized the low, horizontal planes of his prairie houses, forcing the eye of an observer to follow the extensions of the houses out to the flat prairie landscape.

In the dining room of the Willets house, Wright attempted to create a comfortable and meaningful environment for its inhabitants. Wright wrote that he sought to "let walls, ceiling, floors become seen as component parts of each other, their surfaces flowing into each other."

Suddenly on his own after an apprenticeship of nearly six years with Adler & Sullivan, Wright lost no time in opening an office in the Schiller Building, a structure that had been designed by Sullivan. For a while he shared the space with Cecil Corwin, his old friend from Silsbee's firm, and executed his drafting in the Oak Park studio.

At 25, Wright had acquired impressive credentials. He had worked with Silsbee, one of Chicago's most popular architects, and for seven years he had worked alongside Louis Sullivan, one of the key figures in American architecture. Wright had designed 25 buildings, 20 of which

had actually been built (17 houses, the remodeling of a hotel, a school, and a boat house). The Charnley house had brought him considerable praise, and his entry into the widely advertised Milwaukee Public Library and Museum competition in 1893 also helped to publicize his name. If ever there had been a good time to strike out on his own, this was it.

Wright's success during this period was due, in part, to his immense charm and the force of his personality. He had chosen to live in the affluent suburb of Oak Park, and his neighbors—upper-middle-class professionals—certainly appreciated the many parties and social events that he hosted. His son John later remembered the frequent "clam-bakes, tea parties in his studio, cotillions in the large drafting room. . . . From week to week, month to month, our house was a round of parties." In addition to his role as host, Wright avidly participated in community life. He donated money to Oak Park's newspapers, competed in the annual Chicago Horse Show, and was seen at the theater, concerts, museums, and the best restaurants. As a result, Wright met and often enchanted the very people in a position to afford his services. From 1893 through 1901, he produced 71 designs, 49 of which were executed. These included three apartment projects in Chicago, a golf club-house, and several stables and boat houses. During this period, most of his work consisted of private homes in the greater Chicago area and in Wisconsin, where some wealthy Chicagoans spent their summers.

Through designing and building these houses, Wright began to develop his unique philosophy of architecture and his own highly distinctive style. On a technical level, he was deeply concerned with issues of interior space and exterior form. But on a purely emotional level, what concerned him most in these residential commissions was the nature of family life and how to express it in his architecture. How did individual family members function within the house; in what rooms did the family spend time

The Larkin Company Office Building was completed in Buffalo in 1904. The interior, sheltered from the bleak industrial landscape outside, provided a serene work environment.

together; what kinds of rituals were important to them— these were the elusive questions that Wright tried to work out in the arrangement of walls, floors, ceilings, and windows.

Throughout the 1890s, Wright worked slowly and patiently toward blending his technical knowledge with his instinctive grasp of family dynamics. The result—the brilliant formula known as the Prairie Style because Wright designed the houses to harmonize with the flat prairie landscape—first marked him as one of America's great architectural geniuses. Prairie Style houses are characterized by low, wide-eaved roofs; massive chimneys; open porches; garden walls that run directly out from the house (so the house is in effect "married" to the land on which it stands); and rooms that open on to one another without the formal boundaries of walls and doors.

Of these early prairie houses, one of the most significant is the Willets house in Highland Park, built in 1902. With its far-flung porch and porte cochere (a covered carriage entrance), the building seems to stretch out and extend itself across the flat terrain of the prairie, allowing for an easy intermingling of interior and exterior space. Typical of Wright's work at this time are the emphatic horizontals created by the foundations, walls, and rows of casement windows, the low-hipped roof, the centrally placed living room, and the massive chimney. The exterior has a lightness created by ivory stucco and strips of wood that were stained rather than painted. The overall effect is stirring and dynamic, yet, at the same time, supremely restful.

Following the Willets house, Wright received several other important domestic commissions, including the Martin house in Buffalo and the Robie house in Chicago. The Martin house, built in 1904 for the head of the Larkin Soap Company, Darwin D. Martin, is a striking example of the Prairie Style. Its strong horizontal planes are further emphasized by the handsome pergola (arbor or trellis) that leads to the conservatory. Many architectural historians believe that the Robie house, built in 1909, provides the most stunning example of the Prairie Style. A long wall that guards the terrace while still permitting access, along with second- and third-story bedrooms that overlook the street, make the house a strong and sheltering presence that is still very much a part of its neighborhood. As Frederick Robie himself remembered: "I wanted to . . . look out and down the street at my neighbors yet not have them invade my privacy."

Although Wright is remembered chiefly for his residential work during this period, there are two important exceptions. The first of these is the Larkin Building in Buffalo, designed as the headquarters of the Larkin Soap Company. With its imposing brick monoliths, uniform metal furniture, and air conditioning, the Larkin Building created a radical and dazzling vision of modernity when it was built in 1904. The building was demolished in 1950.

Wright's other important nonresidential commission of this period was the Unity Temple of Oak Park. A fire destroyed the original church, giving Wright the opportunity to design a new structure in 1905. Stripped down and stark, the temple owed little to the established conventions of church architecture. In fact, to many people, it scarcely looked like a church at all. But Wright claimed that the room itself was a complete entity, thus symbolizing the unity of God and humanity, an explanation that apparently satisfied his Unitarian clients. While the outside of the structure — made of a pebbly, gray concrete—seems to many observers weighty and enduring, the inside is marvelously spacious and light. The effect from within is one of spiritual harmony and order.

These were busy, active years for Wright, filled with a variety of commissions that enabled him to develop and mature as an architect and as an artist. But one of these commissions, an Oak Park house undertaken for Edwin Cheney and built in 1904, would have far-reaching consequences for his personal life as well. Over the years, Frank's marriage to Catherine had begun to falter, and by this time he could no longer hide the bitter feelings that he held toward her and their life together.

For comfort and solace he turned to his client's wife, Martha Borthwick Cheney, who was known as Mamah (pronounced MAY-mah). Because he was quite well known in the community by this time, his association with her hardly went unnoticed. But Wright had no desire to hide their affair or his intentions. Late in the summer of

(continued on page 57)

The floor plan for the house
shows how Wright broke up the
traditional rigid shape of rooms,
creating wide openings between
rooms that allowed them to flow
freely into each other.

▲ The living room features an exposed brick fireplace and
an inglenook (the bench beside the fireplace). Wright,
who strongly believed in the primacy of family life,
designed most of his residences around large masonry
fireplaces.

◀ Overleaf: The entrance to Frank Lloyd Wright's home in
Oak Park, Illinois, where the architect lived and worked
from 1889 to 1909. The house, a symphony of elementary
geometric shapes, served as a testing ground for many of
Wright's budding architectural theories.

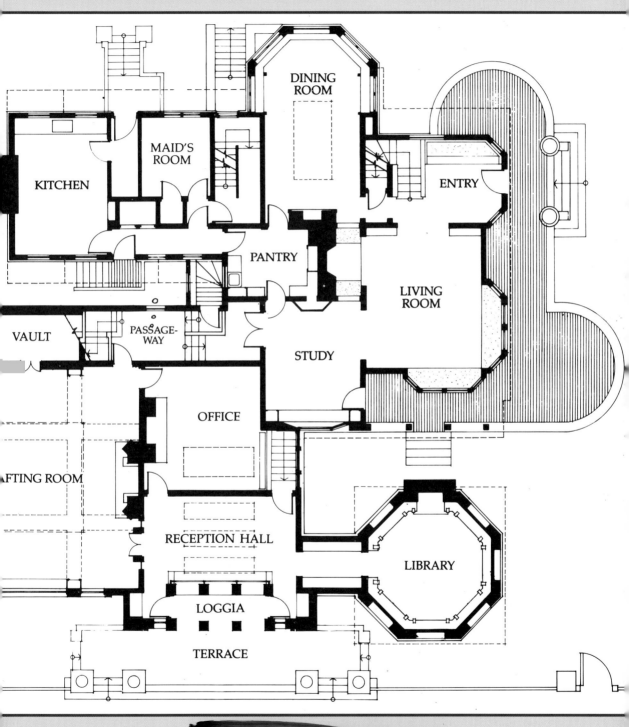

KITCHEN

MAID'S
ROOM

DINING
ROOM

ENTRY

PANTRY

LIVING
ROOM

VAULT

PASSAGE-
WAY

STUDY

OFFICE

FTING ROOM

RECEPTION HALL

LIBRARY

LOGGIA

TERRACE

Light filters into the dining room through bay windows and a patterned ceiling grille. Wright believed that a house and its furnishings should make one integrated design. Here he used natural materials and simple geometric patterns to produce an intimate, earthy environment.

The glass doors and vaulted ceiling in the master bedroom provide a spacious feeling to the small chamber. Wright often quoted the Chinese poet Lao-tzu: "The reality of the building does not consist in the four walls and the roof but in the space within to be lived in."

In the library, Wright extended the octagonal shape of the floor up through the shelves and ceiling trim to the skylights. Wright once wrote, "Whether people are fully conscious of this or not, they actually derive countenance and sustenance from the 'atmosphere' of the things they live in or with."

◀The Wrights conducted family concerts, puppet and magic shows, poetry readings, and parties under the playroom's 18-foot-high barrel-vaulted ceiling. Wright filled the room with dozens of games and toys that he made himself and installed a mural depicting a scene from the Arabian Nights above the fireplace.

By using chain harnesses to eliminate the need for crossties, Wright created a spacious work space in the drafting room of his studio. Wright designed open workrooms in several of his later commercial buildings, such as the Larkin Building and the Johnson Wax offices.

(continued from page 48)

1908, he asked Catherine if she would grant him a divorce. She replied by asking him to wait for a year; if he was still of the same mind, she would then consent to his wishes. But the waiting grew increasingly frustrating, and finally Wright decided to cut the cord. On November 7, 1909, he took matters into his own hands by eloping with Mamah Cheney.

Within the sanctuary of Unity Temple (completed in 1906), Wright used geometric shapes to achieve the ideal interior space.

Wright named Taliesin, his country estate near Spring Green, Wisconsin, after a Welsh poet whose name means "shining brow." Taliesin, which Wright built as a refuge for himself and his mistress Mamah Borthwick, is a personal expression of his theory of organic architecture.

5

Taliesin:
Wright's Shining Brow

BECAUSE WRIGHT HAD BECOME a highly public man, the abrupt desertion of his wife and children became a hot topic of public interest. The press in particular had a field day with the news. Seizing upon a postcard that Catherine wrote to Frank, a large party of reporters went to Oak Park to interview his abandoned mate.

With the company and support of a clergyman, Catherine agreed to meet with reporters and made a long, involved statement that did much to fuel the fires of gossip:

> My heart is with him now. He will come back as soon as he can. I have a faith in Frank Lloyd Wright that passeth understanding, perhaps, but I know him as no one else knows him. . . . His whole life has been a struggle. When he came here as a young architect, he had to fight against every existing idea in architecture. He did fight, year after year, against obstacles that would have downed an ordinary man. He has fought the most tremendous battles. He is fighting one now. I know he will win.

When the same reporters approached Edwin Cheney, his reply was more terse: "I don't care to talk about the matter at all."

But if Edwin Cheney did not want to discuss the matter, it seemed that everyone else in Chicago did. Wright's dramatic decision became the subject of more than one church sermon in the city. For his part, Wright remained insulated from the sea of rumors and gossip. He and Mamah were in Berlin, Germany, where he was consulting with a publisher on a book devoted to his work. He also toured the city but found little to stimulate his architectural interest.

Soon Frank and Mamah decided to leave Berlin, heading south for Florence, Italy, where Frank claimed he felt much more at home. They rented a small villa in the Tuscan town of Fiesole. Once settled, Wright plunged into a study of Italian structures, both humble and grand, including Roman theaters and baths. He also viewed the paintings of the Italian Renaissance master Fra Angelico at the nearby Church of San Domenico. Exhausted from the mental and physical strain of the past few years, Wright spent many hours walking in the villa's high-walled gardens and enjoying the scents of the flowers and pines. The time spent in Italy provided a brief and much-needed period of rest.

But despite Wright's pleasure with his foreign surroundings, he was not entirely at ease with his role as an exile. Deeply American in thought, feeling, and attitude, he yearned to return to the United States and resume his role in conventional society. As 1910 drew to a close, he left Europe and Mamah, setting sail for his homeland.

Upon his return, Frank learned that Catherine still refused to acknowledge the importance of Mamah in his life or to grant him a divorce. Wright's life seemed at a standstill until his mother offered him 200 acres of land that she had inherited as her share of the Lloyd-Jones property near Spring Green, Wisconsin, where he had spent his boyhood. There he began to build a house that he called Taliesin (which means "shining brow" in his ancestors' Welsh language).

In many ways, Taliesin summed up Wright's ideas about architecture. He situated it just below the crest of a hill, beneath which spread a beautiful view of the valley. "No house should be on a hill," he declared. "It should be *of* the hill." Built of the fawn-colored local stone, the original structure had an organic feel and indeed seemed to rise from its natural setting.

Meanwhile, as Wright's dream house took shape, Edwin Cheney granted Mamah a divorce on the grounds of desertion. He retained custody of their two children, although they were allowed to visit their mother periodically. Just before Christmas in 1911, Frank broke the news to reporters that Mamah had joined him at Taliesin. Standing in front of the great fireplace and clad in a scarlet robe, with Mamah sitting close by, Frank read from a prepared statement:

> Let there be no misunderstanding. A Mrs. E. H. Cheney never existed for me, and now is no more in fact. But Mamah Borthwick is here, and I intend to take care of her. ... The solution of this case will be individual, and worked out by honest living, not by patching broken conventions, nursing wounded sensibilities, or hiding behind expediencies. No one will suffer owing to my neglect of any rational obligation, economic or otherwise. .... A written contract does not make a marriage or keep it holy. We depend too much on outward forms and are careless of the spirit beneath them. Integrity of life means unity of thought and feeling and action, and therefore a struggle to square one's life with one's self.

A week later, Wright followed up his flamboyant speech with a written account of the whole incident.

Eventually, all of the commotion died down. News of Wright's domestic affairs slipped from newspaper headlines to the second section and finally ceased to be reported at all. He and Mamah made an effort to withdraw from public scrutiny and concentrated instead on their private life together at Taliesin. Although they kept to themselves, they did not altogether shun contact with their neighbors and tried to establish friendly, if somewhat formal, relationships with them. Wright was still building Taliesin, and he employed local craftsmen and bought his supplies in town. Mamah shopped in Spring Green, and even though heads turned and tongues wagged, she remained composed and friendly. In 1913 and 1914, Wright helped organize a local art exhibit and generously loaned several valuable prints and pieces of pottery. All of these things created within the community an atmosphere of guarded acceptance and tolerance of their untraditional living arrangement.

Between 1911 and 1914, Wright divided his weekdays between his office at Orchestra Hall and a small apartment at 25 East Cedar Street on Chicago's North Side. On weekends he returned to Taliesin and Mamah. Riding back on the train to Madison from Chicago, he made a striking figure in his belted, box-pleated Norfolk jacket, high-laced boots, riding pants, and flowing tie. He usually read from a volume of Shakespeare or Walt Whitman.

From time to time, Wright and Mamah were visited by her son and daughter, who spent most of the year with their father (who had remarried in 1912). Because she was not fully absorbed in the daily responsibilities of motherhood, Mamah found time to pursue various intellectual interests, fostered in part by Frank. She translated a book on free love by the Swiss feminist Ellen Key and made plans to purchase the local weekly newspaper, the *Spring Green Republican*, and to convert it into a mouthpiece of enlightened thought.

Although Frank had settled into a happy home life with Mamah, he was nonetheless beset by constant financial worries. Supporting two households was not easy, and he began a cycle of juggling debts and creditors that often caused him great mental and emotional stress. Through it all, however, he maintained a brave front. If Wright invited

a group of colleagues to dinner at a restaurant and discovered that he could not pay the bill, he thought nothing
of asking his so-called guests to chip in.

Wright also showed himself to be fearless—even bra-
zen—in the presence of his creditors. Once, a sheriff
appeared at his office with an order to lock the place and
seal its contents in judgment for a debt of $1,500. Wright
remained calm and asked for a grace period of 30 minutes,
instructing his son John (who worked for him at the time)
to show the man his drawings. Meanwhile, Wright hurried
over to see a friendly client, who advanced him $10,000.
Wright returned to the office, took the sheriff to a bank to
cash the check, and handed him $1,500. The officer left
with many apologies for having disturbed him. But
Wright's attitude toward money is most clearly revealed
by what happened next. He took the remaining $8,500 and
went shopping with his son. The resulting spree yielded
Wright a fur-lined overcoat, a dozen chairs for Taliesin,
various objects of art, and two grand pianos.

In 1913, a young developer, Edmund Waller, approached Wright about designing Midway Gardens, which
Waller claimed would be "the most beautiful and complete
concert garden in the world." Realizing that he stood to
make a lot of money and receive much recognition for his
contributions, Wright eagerly set to work. He designed
beautifully proportioned rooms, lantern-lighted walkways,
and flowering terraces. There would be a stage for orchestra and ballet performances, a private clubhouse and
restaurant, as well as opera chairs for those who only
wanted to hear the music without the pressure of ordering
food and drink.

While the architecture of the Garden's walls and buildings reflected Wright's continuing preoccupation with
geometric forms, he decided to adorn the building with
sculpture based on the human figure. To this end, he
commissioned Alfonso Iannelli, a well-known sculptor of
the day. His son John Lloyd Wright created an abstract

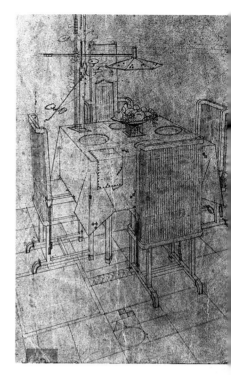

Wright's sketch of the table and place settings for the restaurant at Midway Gardens shows his concern for every design detail of the project. Throughout his career, Wright insisted that all furnishings—including furniture, carpets, and place settings—should be designed as part of the building.

A headline in the August 15, 1914, edition of the Chicago Tribune *reports the horrible tragedy at Taliesin.*

mural placed over the bar, and Waller hired one of the city's leading caterers to handle food services. By the summer of 1914, it seemed that Midway Gardens was going to be a success and that Wright had managed to pull his personal and professional life back together. He was in

no way prepared for what was surely the most horrible tragedy of his life.

On the afternoon of August 14, 1914, Wright was in Chicago hard at work on the Midway Gardens project. At Taliesin, Mamah was enjoying lunch with her two visiting children at a table overlooking a pond. Inside the house, six employees were in the dining room having a meal of their own. As they sat unaware, the recently hired chef, Julian Carleton, poured buckets of gasoline on the kitchen floor and locked the door that led to the courtyard. He then set fire to the room and stationed himself at the exit, using an ax to kill those who tried to escape. He found time to rush to the terrace, where he killed Mamah and the two children.

In Chicago, Wright had just finished lunch when he received a long-distance telephone call from Spring Green saying that Taliesin had been destroyed by fire. He immediately boarded the train for Madison and tried to prepare himself for the worst. Upon arriving home, his fears were confirmed: Mamah, the children, and four others were dead; the house was in ruins.

Edwin Cheney and many of the Spring Green residents who only three years earlier had openly condemned Wright's actions now comforted him. Carleton was captured and held for trial, but an attempt to poison himself before his arrest resulted in his death several weeks later. He never explained what had motivated his brutal acts.

Shattered and sick at heart, Frank had Mamah buried in the little chapel cemetery that was the final resting place for the members of his family. No headstone was set at the grave, for as Wright said, "Why mark the spot where desolation ended and began?" The night after the funeral, Wright had a cot set up in one of the workshops that had escaped destruction and tried to sleep. Years later, he recalled how he was unable to close his eyes that night and instead got up and, dazed by grief and despair, wandered around the ruins of his life.

Architect Frank Lloyd Wright (center) shares a traditional meal with his Japanese associates. Between 1916 and 1922, Wright spent much of his time in Tokyo supervising the construction of the Imperial Hotel.

6

Picking Up the Pieces

THE TRAGEDY AT TALIESIN proved to be a turning point in Wright's life. As his son John later commented, "Something in him died with her . . . something lovable and gentle." But despite, or perhaps because of, this emotionally devastating event, Wright clung fast to his work. "Only architecturally," wrote John, "was he able to hold his own." After completing the details of Midway Gardens in the fall of 1914, Wright began to rebuild his studio and home, which he decided to call Taliesin II. He supervised the cutting of wood and the quarrying of stone as if his very life depended on these activities.

Because Wright was very much a public figure, news of the massacre spread far and wide. As a result, he received hundreds of letters—many from complete strangers—offering condolences and sympathy. At first, he bundled the letters and burned the entire lot. But Wright then worried that he might be destroying correspondence from friends,

Sculptor Miriam Noel (pictured here in 1927) came to Wright's emotional rescue following the tragedy at Taliesin. For more than 12 years, their stormy relationship provided sensational headlines for the tabloids.

so he asked David Robinson, the manager of his Chicago office, to screen the mail before disposing of it. Occasionally, Robinson would show his boss a particularly sympathetic letter because he thought that such unsolicited expressions of kindness might help to lift Wright's spirits.

A woman named Miriam Noel wrote one of the letters that Robinson relayed to Wright. In her letter, she told Wright that she, too, was an artist and could therefore understand his suffering. Something about her words touched him, and he responded to the note. She, in turn, wrote back. When Robinson saw the second letter, he asked Wright if he should put it aside to be burned, but Wright wanted to see it. Miriam Noel suggested that the two meet; she had known her own sorrows and felt that she could offer him useful advice. So Wright invited her to visit.

A few days later, they sat face-to-face at Wright's desk. Although she was no longer young, Miriam Noel remained a strikingly attractive woman. Richly dressed in a sealskin cape, she had pale skin that formed a vivid contrast to her dark red hair. Wright said that he had never met anyone like her. Mrs. Noel told the architect that she was a sculptor. She had lived in Paris until the outbreak of World War I in 1914 forced her to return to the United States. She was divorced from a Kentucky doctor, Thomas Noel, with . whom she had had three children. Utterly charmed, Wright invited her to move into Taliesin shortly after this meeting.

Once she had settled in, Miriam Noel set about attracting as much attention to herself as she possibly could. Like Wright, she exhibited a need to be in the limelight and immediately began issuing public statements about their life together. At a press conference she stated, "Frank Lloyd Wright and I are as capable of making laws of our own as were the dead men who framed the laws by which they hoped to rule the generations that followed them." She and Wright were among the few to achieve the freedom that comes, as Miriam put it, "only through the illumination of the spiritual consciousness." Initially, Wright admired her boldness in expressing her views, which were comparable to his own.

But the relationship between Frank and Miriam, despite their similar temperaments and personal philosophies, proved stormy almost from the start. Demanding and difficult, Miriam wanted all of Frank's time and attention, and she bitterly resented his continuing attachment to the memory of Mamah Borthwick. After living at Taliesin for only nine months, Miriam moved out, taking up residence in Frank's apartment at 25 East Cedar Street in Chicago.

Many of Wright's friends and contemporaries wondered why he did not rid himself of this woman who had become so troublesome. Some friends felt that his insistent need to publicize his private life made it impossible for Frank to renounce Miriam without appearing to go back on his own publicly espoused principles. Others suggested that he had an overwhelming need for female companionship. But whatever the reason, Wright hung on.

At the same time, the building of Taliesin had severely drained Frank's financial resources, and his wife, Catherine, still refused to grant him a divorce. In the midst of this sea of troubles came the welcome offer in 1914 to design and build the Imperial Hotel in Tokyo, for which he would be paid the handsome sum of $300,000.

Wright had first learned of the project a year earlier, when a Japanese delegation visited him during his trip to New York City. Although the Japanese obviously admired his work, Wright thought no more about the commission until it was securely his.

Accompanied by Miriam Noel, Wright left for Tokyo in December 1916 to begin work on the hotel. For the next seven years, the bulk of Wright's time, both personal and professional, was devoted to it, although he had a few other commissions in Japan and the United States during this period. The building of the hotel was marked by many difficulties, both financial and personal. Miriam became a constant source of embarrassment to Frank, upbraiding him publicly and often interrupting when he tried to speak.

Yet despite all these problems, Wright did not falter, and the hotel gradually assumed its shape and form. A vast, broad-winged, tawny structure of lava and brick, the Imperial Hotel presented many challenges to its creator. One of his paramount concerns in designing the building was protecting the hotel from the earthquakes that periodically shook the city and demolished its buildings. Wright devised a technique for the structure to absorb shocks by sinking the central supports into soft earth so that the floor slabs would be held up "as a waiter balances a tray on his fingers." He had seen how the railroad stations and office buildings in Chicago were supported on piers sunk into the sludge beneath the Loop (a district in the heart of downtown Chicago), and he was firmly convinced that the Imperial Hotel required a similar technique.

Although many of Wright's critics called the hotel a masterpiece, others were less convinced. Some complained that the interior space was confusing and disorienting; others felt that the windows were placed too high on the bedroom walls. A businessman from Tennessee sniffed, "I never in my life paid so much money for a room

Wright's original sketch of the Imperial Hotel shows the magnitude of the structure. In the design for the building, he managed to combine Western construction techniques with Eastern aesthetics, incorporating such elements as inner gardens and templelike motifs.

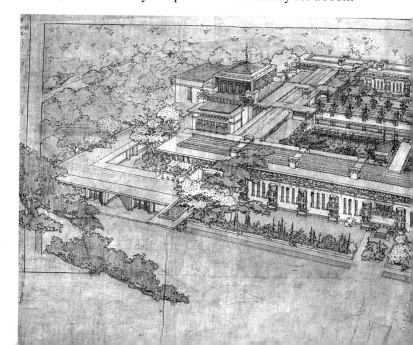

I couldn't see out of." Of the overall effect, another American caustically remarked, "Fascinating, ingenious and unique are the words that leap to the mind; the same are probably equally applicable to a rabbit warren." Yet the extravagant, ornate structure manages to combine Western construction techniques with Eastern aesthetics in a way that remains compelling. When the hotel later managed to resist the impact of a major earthquake, Wright's accomplishment received international acclaim.

While still actively involved with the construction of the Imperial Hotel, Wright made several trips between Japan and the United States. He executed an important commission for Aline Barnsdall, a California oil heiress. The large concrete structure, called Hollyhock House because of its stylized floral decorations patterned after the hollyhock (Barnsdall's favorite flower), brought Wright many troubles. "This is worse than Japan," he said, referring to the lengthy haggling with contractors and with his client's friends, who freely criticized the house.

These problems paled in comparison with those Wright encountered while working on another important California commission, La Miniatura, in Pasadena. Wright's client, Alice Millard, had commissioned one of the first

prairie houses when she lived in Chicago with her husband, George, a bookstore executive. After her husband died, Millard decided to move to California and wanted Wright to build her new home.

On the surface, the match seemed ideal because Millard was already familiar with his work and trusted his ideas. In La Miniatura, Wright first employed the process of filling hollow, precast concrete blocks with poured concrete. These blocks could be cast to include geometric patterns that enlivened the entire surface of the building. But difficulties arose when the contractor began spending all of his time building a new house for himself while the costs for La Miniatura continued to escalate. Wright and Millard pursued legal action, but the house remained incomplete. When it finally was finished in 1923, a rainstorm nearly washed away the house, which was situated in a ravine that turned into a riverbed when the rains came. During the next downpour, the roof began to leak, but that fault turned out to be the result of substandard waterproofing rather than any failure in Wright's design.

When Wright left Japan for good in November 1922, the hotel remained unfinished. During the time that he spent there, Wright was often sick, physically exhausted, and emotionally drained. Miriam remained at his side, but her presence proved more of an irritant than a comfort. Wright's frequent trips across the Pacific Ocean to oversee projects in Japan and California sapped his strength. And he was deeply disturbed by the growing animosity between the United States and Japan. He was more than ready to leave the country and return to Taliesin for a rest.

After a relaxing ocean voyage home, Wright felt renewed in spirit. He told reporters who interviewed him at the Congress Hotel in Chicago, "I shall rest at Taliesin and decide whether to make the headquarters of my work in Los Angeles or Chicago." Frank also learned that Catherine was finally willing to agree to the divorce that he had sought for so long.

Although Wright was free to marry Miriam Noel, he waited another year before formalizing their union in November 1923 in a strange midnight ceremony on a bridge overlooking the Wisconsin River. Many observers have speculated about his willingness to bind himself to a woman whom he had battled and been unhappy with for years. According to his son John, Wright had been "wooed, grabbed and bagged . . . dominated, seduced, coerced, chastised, conscripted, overridden, and beshawed" by Miriam. Certainly her published letters reveal an attitude toward Wright that was filled with venom and show a tendency to exaggerate or even distort the facts of their life together. She claimed that Taliesin, where Wright's mother also lived, was a den of orgies and debauchery and that Wright frequently assaulted her.

Some observers have suggested that Wright married her simply to calm what was rapidly turning to hysteria. And he may have felt a certain loyalty for this troubled woman who appeared in his hour of need and stayed with him

Wright drew this sketch for Hollyhock House, a residence he designed in Hollywood, California, for oil heiress Aline Barnsdall. The large concrete building, completed in 1920, reminded some observers of the designs of ancient Mayan temples and Wright's own Imperial Hotel.

through periods when he was a professional and social outcast. She had also given him money to rebuild Taliesin, which may have been another reason Wright felt indebted to her.

Whatever Frank's motives for marrying Miriam, the act did nothing to quiet her increasingly troubled spirit, and in

Wright first used the process of filling hollow, precast concrete blocks with poured concrete in La Miniatura (1923), a house that he built in Pasadena, California. The blocks, which could be cast to include geometric designs, were strung together with reinforced steel rods.

April 1924, a mere five months after the wedding, she left him once again. During the next year, Wright seemed to be marking time until he could decide upon his next major move. Meanwhile, his old mentor Louis Sullivan died in 1925 in poverty and obscurity in Chicago. Wright and Sullivan had renewed their friendship and maintained a correspondence in which they discussed the future of organic architecture. Deeply saddened by the event, he wrote two articles in commemoration of his *Lieber Meister*. Although he secured several more commissions in California, Wright announced that his headquarters would be located in Chicago and that he planned to devote himself exclusively to commercial architecture.

These plans, however, were destined for failure. Defective telephone wiring started a fire that ravaged Taliesin II, causing between $250,000 and $500,000 worth of damage. With only $30,000 in insurance, Wright reluctantly sold his Oak Park home for $35,000 to raise cash to rebuild Taliesin.

As if that were not bad enough, Miriam announced that she planned to sue Wright for divorce, charging that he beat her on two occasions. Frank, eager to be done with her, offered Miriam a lump sum of $10,000, with an additional $250 a month for the rest of her life, which she refused to accept. Miriam's suit provided the press with their first knowledge of the separation and, for that matter, of the marriage. Reporters descended on Spring Green, and Wright's personal life once again made headlines.

A new scoop about Wright even managed to surpass the story about Miriam—the wholly unexpected revelation that the 59-year-old Wright had taken up with yet another female companion—this time, a 26-year-old divorcée by the name of Olga Iovanovna Lazovich Milanoff Hinzenberg. Once again, Wright had managed to confound and surprise the public with his highly unconventional behavior.

Olgivanna Wright, Frank's third wife, posed for this portrait in 1931. Frank met Olgivanna, 33 years his junior, in 1924 and married her 4 years later. She remained his devoted companion for the rest of his life.

7

Troubled Times

OLGA MILANOFF, or Olgivanna, as she was called, was the daughter of the chief justice of Montenegro (a republic of Yugoslavia) and the granddaughter of a venerated general. Privately educated in Russia and Turkey, she married Vlademar Hinzenberg, a Russian architect 10 years her senior, while still in her teens. In 1917, she gave birth to a daughter, Svetlana, but left her husband shortly thereafter and went to Paris, where she pursued her interests—art and mysticism.

While on a brief visit to Chicago to see Hinzenberg on business, she attended a performance of the Russian ballet. Wright, who was at the theater with his friend Jerome Blum, spotted her and guessed that she was foreign. During the intermission, Blum approached her, asking if perhaps they had met before. It seemed they had, at the home of a mutual acquaintance. Blum then introduced Wright. Although she had never heard of him, Olgivanna graciously acknowledged the introduction and accepted Frank's offer to join him for tea at the nearby Congress Hotel after the performance.

According to Wright, Olgivanna's dark good looks and haunting, aristocratic manner captivated him immediately. By the end of the tea, he believed himself to be in love with the lady. Through invitations to Spring Green and visits to New York, he wooed her ardently, and before long he proclaimed that "Olgivanna [is] mine." She moved into Taliesin II in February 1925 and finalized a divorce with her husband a mere two months later. Before the end of the year, she had given birth to the couple's daughter, whom they called Iovanna. Once again, the press had a field day.

Some of Wright's biographers have suggested that the women in his life grew less conventional and less willing to assume the customary roles that society had established for them. Certainly this was most true of Olgivanna, who had spent much time in Paris studying with Soviet occult teacher Georgi Gurdjieff at his academy, the Institute for the Harmonious Development of Man. Gurdjieff taught his followers that civilization had corrupted the primordial harmony between the intellectual, physical, and emotional faculties of humans. By adhering to a strict regimen of fasting, physical labor, contemplation, and self-observation, anyone, he declared, could once again be unified in body and spirit.

Gurdjieff's ideas enraptured Frank, and he admired Olgivanna for her willingness to devote herself to them. But beyond being beautiful and exotic, Olgivanna turned out to be loyal, sensible, and smart. Their marriage was strong and durable, and Olgivanna remained Frank's faithful companion and helpmate for the rest of his life.

Olgivanna's feelings for Frank, however, were severely tried, especially in their first years together, when they were continually harassed by the increasingly erratic actions of Miriam Noel. First, Noel began divorce proceedings but then abruptly halted them. She confided all her personal grievances against Wright to a flock of reporters who encouraged her to make shocking statements about him. One day she would agree to a settlement; the next, she would change her mind.

She continued to press her case with the newspapers, claiming that she was penniless, sick, alone, and without a home. "I am still his wife and Taliesin is still my home," she told reporters. "If I can have just a corner of the bungalow to myself I will be satisfied." But it was clear that she wanted more than a corner when she attempted to take over Taliesin by force, smashing a window with a rock and verbally abusing one of Wright's grown daughters who had come out of the house to calm her.

As if Wright did not have enough problems, yet another destructive fire broke out at Taliesin in the spring of 1925, this time caused by defective electrical wiring. He estimated the damage at $200,000. Severely strained by the fire and the financial worries posed by Miriam, Frank nonetheless began plans for building Taliesin III.

But he found it difficult to concentrate when faced with the constant volley of assaults from Miriam, which grew more extreme and vindictive in their nature. She continued to pursue Wright ferociously, tying up all his financial assets and claiming that she would never grant him a divorce. Evidently, she intended to punish him for his association with Olgivanna.

To that end, she allied herself with Hinzenberg, Olgivanna's former husband, and persuaded him to sue Wright for alienation of affections and for custody of nine-year-old Svetlana on the grounds that Olgivanna was an unfit mother. Warrants for the arrests of Wright and Olgivanna were posted, forcing the couple to go into hiding. Rumor had it that they had taken off for Mexico, but they were discovered in a small cabin beside a Minnesota lake. After a humiliating night spent in a county jail, they were released but could not leave the state to return to Taliesin.

Finally, Miriam's venom began to backfire, and public opinion turned against her. Wright's son John and ex-wife Catherine publicly announced that they would do anything in their power to assist him, and several prominent people,

In 1924, Soviet occult teacher Georgi Gurdjieff stands on the deck of a ship carrying him to the United States. Olgivanna studied at Gurdjieff's Institute for the Harmonious Development of Man in Paris. Wright was intrigued by Gurdjieff's ideas, and he supported Olgivanna's adherence to the occultist's techniques.

including the poet Carl Sandburg and Robert Morse Lovett, the editor of the *New Republic*, urged that all charges against him be dropped. After securing visiting rights with Svetlana, Hinzenberg withdrew his case against his ex-wife and Wright. And in a well-timed bid for public sympathy, Frank and Olgivanna published an article in Madison's *Capitol Times* describing Miriam's behavior in all of its appalling detail.

Even Miriam's lawyer, Arthur D. Cloud, resigned from the case in disgust after she had turned down three successive settlements he had arranged. In parting, he stated: "I wanted to be a lawyer, and Mrs. Wright wanted me to be an avenging angel. So I got out. Mrs. Wright is without funds. The first thing to do is get her some money by a temporary but definite adjustment pending a final disposition of the case. But every time I suggested this to her, Mrs. Wright turned it down and demanded that I go out and punish Mr. Wright. I am an attorney, not an instrument of

Even after granting Frank a divorce in 1927, Miriam Noel continued to harass her ex-husband until she was convicted of breaking into his rented house in La Jolla, California, in July 1928.

vengeance." Miriam, however, seemed unperturbed about Cloud's defection and immediately hired another attorney.

Miriam eventually recognized that her case was weakening. After three years of hounding Wright by every legal and personal means available to her, she agreed to a divorce on August 25, 1927. She received a lump sum of $6,000 in cash and a $30,000 trust fund from which she was able to draw $250 a month for the rest of her life. Days later, several of Wright's friends organized Wright, Incorporated, a corporation that was authorized to issue $75,000 in stock and assume control of his finances and estate. Flat broke at this point, Wright was forced to sell shares in himself against his future earning power.

Unfortunately, Miriam's harassment and strange behavior did not end with the signing of the divorce papers. She tried to convince the Immigration and Naturalization Service to deport Olgivanna and chased Wisconsin governor Fred R. Zimmerman around the kitchen of a Chicago hotel in an effort to enlist his aid in arresting Wright for violating his divorce stipulation. In July 1928, she broke into Wright's rented home in La Jolla, California, and smashed up several hundred dollars' worth of furniture. She was given a 30-day suspended sentence, after which she mercifully disappeared from Wright's life.

Wright was now a broken man financially; because he was unable to pay the Bank of Wisconsin money he owed them, his artworks, personal possessions, and machinery were put up for auction. Nevertheless, he remained optimistic about his future. Frank married Olgivanna on August 25, 1928, and they honeymooned in Arizona. The couple then returned to Taliesin, which had been redeemed by the stockholders of Wright, Incorporated. Once back in his beloved home, Wright was able to turn his attention to his work, which had been brought to a painful standstill by the troubles in his personal life, and to the astute vision that propelled him once more toward new—and what some believed to be his greatest—architectural achievements.

*In Falling Water (1936), Wright achieved a creative marriage be-
tween architecture and nature. He situated the house across a stream
at the precipice of a small waterfall; its cantilevered terraces seem to
take flight in every direction. One of the most famous private residences in the world, Falling Water is now a public museum.*

8

The Tide Turns Again

AFTER FRANK AND OLGIVANNA WERE MARRIED, he quickly sent friends in Chicago the following telegram: "We Are Altogether Well and Happy Going to Put New Life into New Buildings in the Great Arizona Desert Spaces During the Next Year or So." He was enormously moved by the dramatic western landscapes and eager to make his mark upon them. But despite Wright's grand intentions, very few of his Arizona commissions were executed. A summer colony for Lake Tahoe, which included wooden buildings and houseboats with a leaf-and-tepee motif, was never built. San Marcos-in-the-Desert, a winter resort, was carefully planned, but the large-scale concrete block design never left the drawing board.

In the period from 1924 through 1936, years in which many Americans suffered from the economic hardships of the Great Depression, Wright built very few projects. Yet this was hardly a fallow time; the seeds of some of his finest future creations lay in many of his unexecuted plans. For example, the 1929 project for the vestry tower of St.

In 1928, the Wrights head out for New York City in their roadster. Wright maintained a cottage (background) in Ocatilla, Arizona, and he began building Taliesin West, his desert residence near Phoenix, Arizona, in 1938.

Mark's-in-the-Bouwerie, an apartment building for downtown New York City, became the model for the Price Tower, built in 1953 in Bartlesville, Oklahoma. The spiral automobile ramp designed for Sugar Loaf Mountain, an elaborate tourist facility in Maryland, was later used for the Solomon R. Guggenheim Museum in New York City, and the valley-leaping arches of the Edward H. Doheny ranch development were ultimately realized in the Marin County Civic Center buildings in 1959.

Because Wright remained in severe financial straits and had no immediate prospects for new clients, he turned elsewhere to make his living. An opinionated and articulate spokesman, he enthusiastically wrote about and lectured on his architectural theories. From 1929 to 1932, he published more than 20 articles, speeches, and reviews. He was also the subject of many interviews in the general and professional press. His 1930 lectures at Princeton University and at the Art Institute of Chicago were published the next year as *Modern Architecture* and *Two Lectures on Architecture*.

In September 1931, Wright gave a series of informal talks at the New School for Social Research in New York City in which he advocated the improvement of sky-scrapers, lauded industrial architecture, and vehemently attacked urban planning and the International Style of architecture. (The International Style, practiced by such notable architects as Le Corbusier and Ludwig Mies van der Rohe, consciously avoided previous styles. At the time, it was considered the vanguard of modern architecture, and the movement dominated the field for most of the 20th century.) The next year, Wright published *The Disappearing City*, an analysis of urbanization and geographic centralization. After this came *An Autobiography* (1933), a thoroughly fascinating, although error-filled, account of his life up to that point.

Because Wright was so outspoken in his criticism of American life and art, he often appeared in the popular media, stating his opinion on a wide range of topics, even those about which he had little knowledge. Many people felt that the architect, now in his late sixties, was an eccentric, arrogant old man whose productive and creative life was well behind him. But in his characteristic way, Wright soon proved the public wrong once again.

The first major sign of Wright's comeback was the establishment of the Taliesin Fellowship, a self-styled school in which he planned to train students in the fundamental principles of "essential architecture" along with "Philosophy, Sculpture, Painting, Music and the Industrial Crafts." The fellows, handpicked by Wright, would undergo "a direct work experience" in which apprenticeship rather than scholarship would be emphasized.

Wright originally intended to instruct 70 apprentices at Taliesin. But he soon realized that the property could not house more than 23 at a time, so he cut back the admissions. When the fellowship embarked upon its first year on October 1, 1932, every spot was filled, forcing Wright to establish a waiting list for the hopeful applicants whom he was unable to accept.

The apprentices spent their time immersed in a program of work and study that Wright had carefully devised. For three hours each day, they worked on Taliesin contruction projects or labored in the fields, kitchen, laundry, and barns. As Wright put it, the farm and the garden were to be "so managed to employ the help of the apprenticeship that a substantial portion of the living of members may come from their own labor on the grounds, thus enabling the apprentice fees to remain as low as possible." As low as possible meant, at the start, the sum of $1,100. When they were not working, apprentices studied "organic" design or applied themselves to painting, philosophy, or drama. They also studied molding, casting, woodworking, and typography.

Initially, living quarters were located at Taliesin itself, but they were later moved to the nearby Hillside Home School. Under Wright's direction, the apprentices added to and remodeled this building. They converted the old gymnasium into a playhouse and built a large drafting room–dormitory, additional dormitories, dining room, kitchen, and galleries. The entire complex was completed in 1939.

As soon as the playhouse was finished in November 1933, Wright opened it to the general public and charged 50 cents admission. Visitors could watch a foreign film, munch doughnuts and sip tea with Olgivanna, and converse with Wright himself. After 1934, Wright began apprentice-conducted tours of Taliesin, again charging 50 cents. He also solicited contributions from friends, former clients, and patrons of the arts. Architectural giants Walter Gropius and Ludwig Mies van der Rohe were among the financial contributors.

Many people criticized the Taliesin Fellowship, charging that Wright offered little more than a chance to pay for the "privilege" of doing hard labor and sustaining his property. But the applicants who sought selection to the fellowship viewed the matter differently. To them, Wright was the brilliant sun around which all activity revolved; the students were eager to be in his presence morning, noon, and night. Applications poured in from all over the world, and apprentices hailed from China, Egypt, Greece, India, Holland, Italy, Japan, Mexico, and Venezuela as well as from the United States.

As the fellowship evolved, Olgivanna suggested, and Wright agreed, that servants were vulgar and had no place at Taliesin. Thus, apprentices were asked to set the tables, serve the meals, and rise at 2:00 A.M. to start the fires in the kitchen. Because the domestic chores (like all others at the fellowship) rotated, the apprentices took their turns serving the master and, at other times, joining his table for a meal and the elevated pleasure of his conversation.

Some biographers have criticized Wright's role as the grand master of Taliesin, charging that the fellowship was not a true coming together of equals but a strict hierarchy in which Wright needed to outshine everyone else. He permitted no criticism of his work either by students or instructors, and he was never readily challenged. Some have said that as a result the atmosphere at Taliesin was provincial, isolated, and ingrown.

Yet Wright was a dynamic and charismatic presence at Taliesin, and he offered his students a unique method of learning their craft. He was constantly expounding his philosophy at spontaneous moments throughout the day as well as during the regular discussions that followed break-fast on Sunday mornings. In these talks, he often emphasized the importance of nature to the architect's vision.

Once, Wright delivered an impromptu lesson with a tray of seashells to illustrate his point. He noted how although shells housed a lower order of life, their shapes nevertheless displayed an abundance of originality and invention. Each shell was different, and this "multitudinous expression indicates what design can mean." He went on to add:

"There is no reason why our buildings and the housing of
human beings, which we so stupidly perpetrate all alike as
two peas in a pod, shouldn't be quite as fertile in imagina-
tive resource as these little seashells. Why do we ever take
any one formula, carry it out to a dead end, and execute it
as though that were all? Here in this collection of little
houses is one of the best lessons you could possibly find.
Study them."

One could argue that Wright did more than train young
architects at Taliesin; he also created disciples for his
ideas. This may have indirectly led to his resurgence as a
prominent architect. Through an apprentice, Edgar Kaufmann, Jr., Wright received a commission for a house that
put his name in the forefront of American architecture once
more. Falling Water, as the structure is known, is one of
the most famous modern houses in the world.

When Kaufmann entered the fellowship in 1934, Wright
was undertaking very few commissions. The young apprentice, however, was very impressed with Wright's
talents and urged his father to give the master a commission. The senior Kaufmann, a Pittsburgh department store
owner, needed an architect to design his weekend retreat
in Connellsville, Pennsylvania. Conceding to the pleas of
his son, Kaufmann assigned the job to Wright.

Wright's Falling Water, asserts biographer Robert C.
Twombly, destroys assumptions of what a house can and
should be and do. Wright devoted most of its floor space
to a massive living room—as well as terraces, walls, and
canopy slabs that shoot out in all four directions. The
kitchen, baths, and three bedrooms occupy a relatively
small portion of the overall space. Contemporary architectural historians believe that pictures of the finished house
are inadequate because they cannot convey the way in
which it seems to take flight every which way at once.

The most remarkable aspect of Falling Water is the way
it exploits the site on which it is built. Two deeply cantilevered terraces seem to hover in space without visible

means of support. Horizontal sweeps of reinforced concrete and the vertical thrust of the glass-and-stone fireplace anchor the house firmly to its rocky plateau and, at the same time, echo the dramatic plunge of ledge and stream. Overhanging roofs, far-flung cantilevers, and outreaching walls tie the house to the site, yet never restrict it.

Twombly also suggests that Wright achieved a brilliant balance between architecture and nature in Falling Water; never had he demonstrated better how a structure should be *of* its surroundings than he did in this forceful synthesis of opposites. At once stable and floating, Falling Water is both linked to the spot on which it is built, yet at the same time it seems to leap off the ground into space. Fluid and inflexible, static and dynamic, permanent and ever changing, Falling Water is Wright's nature poem to modern humanity and all its complex, contradictory impulses.

While Falling Water was clearly a luxury structure designed for a wealthy merchant, Wright did not ignore the

The interior of Falling Water produces a relaxing atmosphere befitting a country retreat. Wright fervently believed that architects had the sacred obligation to build structures that were appropriate, natural, and above all, beautiful in relation to the needs of their inhabitants.

other end of the economic spectrum, especially during the
depression era. His other great achievement during the
1930s was the development of the more modestly priced
Usonian house. (*Usonia* was the term that English writer
Samuel Butler used to denote the United States in his
futuristic 1917 novel *Erewhon*.) Wright designed the
Usonian house to provide the average modern family with
affordable, quality housing—costing about $5500 in 1937.

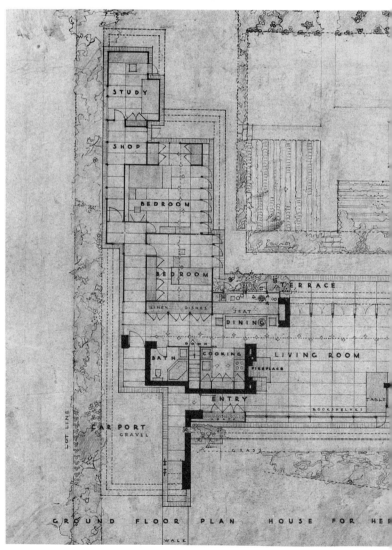

To keep the price down, Wright employed many innovative architectural economies in the Usonian house.
The concrete slab foundation rested on a drained bed of
cinders and sand. Hot-water pipes that were placed under
the foundation produced "gravity," or radiant heat, which
rose through the floor and eliminated the need for ducts
and radiators. The insulated slab roof housed the ventila-
tion system, and its extra long overhangs protected the

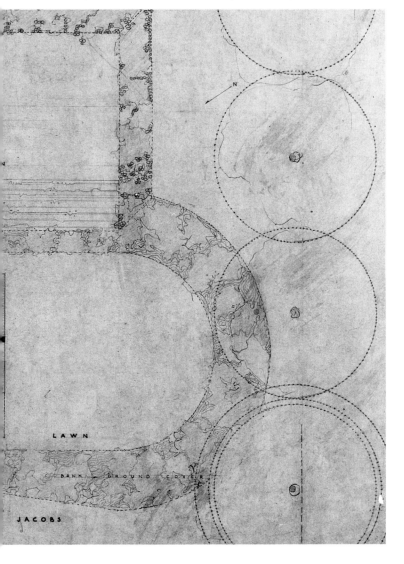

*The floor plan for the Her-
bert Jacobs house (1937),
Wright's first Usonian
house. He designed Uso-
nian houses to provide the
average modern family
with affordable quality
housing. Wright's design
and innovative use of ma-
terials to save money influenced the development of
prefabricated houses.*

exterior. The ready-made walls, which were raised in horizontal panels assembled at the building site, consisted of three layers of boards and two layers of heavy-duty tar paper pressed together. The assembly and the insulation of the house cost considerably less than the more conventional methods of the day.

The first Usonian house to be constructed was the 1937 Jacobs house. Here Wright demonstrated innovation in the design as well as the technology. He eliminated the dining room, replacing it with a table alcove connecting the kitchen and living area, which gave the effect of three rooms merging into one. To safeguard privacy, Wright turned the house away from the street, so that its only visible windows were a series of small openings that ran under the overhanging roof. But the living room, which faced the interior lot, was lined with more than 20 feet of floor-to-ceiling windows and doors that led out to the terrace. L-shaped glass was wrapped around the outside corner of one of the bedrooms so that during the winter the sun provided enough light and heat to reduce fuel costs significantly. In the summer, the sun crossed overhead without shining directly into the room.

Wright included other design innovations in the Jacobs house, such as the use of glass, stained wood, and brick walls in order to eliminate the need for paint, varnish, plaster, and wallpaper. In place of a cellar, Wright tripled storage space with a row of closets running the length of the outside wall of the bedroom corridor. Holes piercing the house's roof overhangings conducted rainwater into drains in the foundation slab, eliminating gutters and downspouts. He replaced the garage with a carport that was walled on only two sides and connected to the front entry. Wright removed doors from kitchen cabinets, abolished light fixtures and radiators, and designed much of the furniture himself.

Herbert Jacobs was very pleased with the result, and he later hired Wright to design a second home when his family outgrew the first one. In *An Autobiography* (second edition, 1943), Wright claims that he designed 26 more Usonian homes between 1937 and 1943. While this figure may be somewhat inflated, the Usonian house had gained immense popularity in the late 1930s and early 1940s. With its single floor, bedroom wing, glass-faced patio, carport, open plan, and generous window space, the Usonian house became a prototype of the modern American ranch home and rekindled widespread public interest in Wright's work.

In 1938, Wright instructs four of his fellowship apprentices in the studio at Taliesin III.

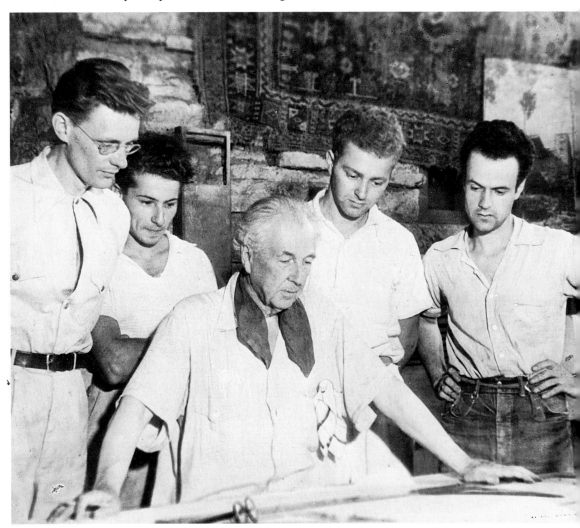

Wright chats with 3 well-wishers at a party celebrating his 89th birthday in 1956. Throughout his life, Wright invited guests from a wide range of professions to his home to ensure a fresh flow of ideas.

9

A Grand Old Man

THE ACCOMPLISHMENTS OF WRIGHT'S LAST YEARS were not confined to residential commissions. Around the time that Falling Water was being finished, he received an offer to design the administration building for the Johnson Wax Company in Racine, Wisconsin. Herbert F. Johnson, head of the company, originally discussed the project with another architect but changed his mind after hearing some of Wright's ideas for the project.

Johnson went to see Wright at Taliesin, but the two men did not get along very well. Johnson offended Olgivanna by criticizing the food he was served; when he showed Wright pictures of the company's old office, Wright plainly told him he thought it looked awful. Yet somehow Wright's prickly manner intrigued Johnson. He would later write: "If that guy can talk like that, he must have something." Johnson followed his hunch and gave the commission to Wright.

Wright quickly made the trip to Racine, where he tried to convince Johnson to move the entire plant out of the city and into the surrounding

Wright consults with his client, Herbert Johnson, during the construction of the Johnson Wax Administration Building (1936–39) in Racine, Wisconsin.

countryside, with a model town for employees encircling it. Johnson, who was already making a bold move in hiring Wright rather than the more conventional architect he had first approached, refused to consider the suggestion seriously. Nevertheless, Wright's design contained enough innovations to satisfy even the most avant-garde architect.

Wright threw himself into the project with a feverish intensity. In *An Autobiography* he describes his reaction to the news of getting the commission: "The birds began to sing again below the house at Taliesin; dry grass on the hillside turned green, and the hollyhocks went gaily into a second blooming. . . . What a release of energy—the making of those plans! Ideas came tumbling up and out onto paper."

Indeed, Wright completed the basic drawings for the building in the astonishingly short period of 10 days. Johnson was delighted at first, but his euphoria soon faded when he began to understand that the new building would be subject to Wright's very expensive habit of refining his original ideas during construction. Wright originally promised that the structure and its interior furnishings would cost a quarter of a million dollars, but by the time it was erected in 1939, that figure had risen to nearly $3 million.

The completed building perfectly reflected the Johnson family's attitudes toward the workplace and their employees. Unlike the large impersonal corporations that were beginning to dominate the U.S. business scene, the Johnson Wax Company maintained a strong personal involvement with its workers and sought to instill in them a close family feeling. To this end, Wright designed the administration building as an enclosed unit that effectively

In the Johnson Wax Administration Building (right), completed in 1939, and the Laboratory Tower (left), completed in 1950, Wright used rounded corners and streamlined surfaces to produce fresh, modernistic buildings.

For the interior of the Johnson Wax Administration Building, Wright created the Great Workroom, a large, airy space crowned by a balcony containing executive offices. Slender, graceful columns that resemble giant white lily pads rise from the workroom floor and become the roof; natural light streams down through glass tubing between the pads.

shuts out the structure's shabby industrial surroundings. Even the main entrance leads to a covered parking lot, enhancing the self-contained nature of the structure.

Inside, the building's large, windowless brick rectangle is lit by both skylights and two strips of translucent Pyrex tubing—one encircling the structure just below the roof line and the other a few feet above eye level. The main office space is a single large room (20 x 128 x 228 feet), ringed by a balcony. Indirect lighting, rich textures, and a scattering of tall, graceful pillars create an atmosphere of warmth and intimacy unusual for such a busy office space.

Robert C. Twombly points out that the organization of the Johnson Wax Building reinforces the traditional ideas about the relationship of labor to management. The pres-

ident's suite is at the top of the structure, at the juncture of the two oval penthouses that contain the other offices. Below them, on the balcony level, are the offices of the junior executives and the department heads. Farther below, in the large main room, the clerical staff is grouped together where their superiors can easily watch over them.

Johnson and his employees found the results more than satisfying. Wright had attempted to create a building "as beautiful to live and work in as any cathedral was to worship in," and he evidently succeeded. Efficiency increased dramatically in the new surroundings, and many employees began to come in early and stay late, preferring the pleasant office to their often unattractive dwellings.

The construction of the Johnson Wax Building reinvigorated Wright. He exuded optimism and confidence in the project, often climbing around the scaffolds with the energy of a man half his age. Old friends thought he looked younger during this time than he had 10 years earlier.

One of his finest moments on the project came when it was time to test the 24-foot concrete columns with which he planned to support the roof of the main workroom. These columns had the appearance of giant water-lily pads. ("But of course!" Wright had said. "My vocabulary and nature's are one. To be in the Great Workroom is to be among pine trees, breathing fresh air and sunlight.") The building license authorities were skeptical about the ability of the slender, tapering columns to hold up their calculated load of six tons each. So Wright announced that he would publicly test a sample column. Such a boisterous crowd of people showed up to witness the testing that police had to erect barricades to keep them from overrunning the area.

Wright put on a terrific show, directing the crane as it dropped ton after ton of scrap metal on the wide top of the column. Sixty tons were heaped on the column before it finally collapsed, establishing beyond a shadow of a doubt that the column could easily hold its six-ton weight. After the success of this building, Wright went on to design a supplementary research tower in 1946 and a large house for Johnson and his new wife, called Wingspread, located a few miles north of Racine.

Partly because of the overwhelmingly positive reaction to the Johnson Wax Building, Wright's reputation was once again on the rise. In 1938, the magazine *Architectural Forum* devoted an entire issue to his work, and in the same year, *Time* magazine called him the nation's greatest architect. Favorable coverage in such publications as *Saturday Review*, *Scientific American*, the *Christian Science Monitor*, the *New Republic*, and *Newsweek* soon followed.

Finally, Wright's genius began to be recognized and honored throughout the world. The Royal Institute of British Architects awarded Wright a gold medal (1939), he was inducted into the National Academy of Architects in both Uruguay (1941) and Mexico (1942), and he was invited to represent the United States at the International Convention of Architects in Moscow (1937). On the domestic scene, he received honorary degrees from Wesleyan, Yale, Princeton, and the University of Wisconsin. The Museum of Modern Art in New York City held an extensive retrospective of Wright's work from November 1940 to January 1941, and he was featured in the Masters of Four Arts Exhibition at Harvard's Fogg Museum along with French sculptor Aristide Maillol, Spanish painter Pablo Picasso, and Russian composer Igor Stravinsky.

During the 1940s, Wright spent much of his time traveling and disseminating his ideas throughout the United States. He never hesitated to criticize what he saw. He called the buildings in Los Angeles "a dish of tripe" and those of New England "fire-traps" and "vermin catchers." In Chicago, he derided developers for chopping up land into tiny housing lots and called the buildings in the nation's capital "symbols of authority out of a pontifical past."

But Wright did not always complain. Ever enchanted by the Great American Desert, he had bought 800 acres of

land in Paradise Valley near Phoenix, Arizona, when his practice began to revive in the 1930s. Eventually, he designed and built Taliesin West. The first structure of this second home, the drafting room, is made of desert stone and redwood and has a white canvas roof that diffuses the light. Side flaps open to the wind to dispel the arid heat. Later buildings employed multicolored stone and redwood and were set off by green irrigated gardens and deep blue pools.

Like its precursor, Taliesin West harmonized with its surroundings. Built low to the ground, constructed of native materials, and landscaped with local vegetation, it was perfectly suited to the hot, dry climate in which it was situated. Taliesin West became the winter home of the fellowship. Apprentices went there in the fall and remained until the following spring. Wright traveled back and forth between his two residences in grand style, usually driven in shifts by apprentices in one of his many cars. Years later, he was transported by airplane.

Although by now an old man, Wright remained vigorous, actively pursuing important new commissions. For example, the Price Tower in Bartlesville, Oklahoma,

Taliesin West, Wright's camp in Arizona, rises majestically from the desert landscape. A brilliant blend of indigenous materials, colors, patterns, and textures, the sprawling complex reflects Wright's characteristic use of shapes and materials that are perfectly suited to the function and setting of the building.

enabled him to resurrect the aborted designs for the tower of St. Mark's-in-the Bouwerie. Called the most romantic structure in the country, the Price Tower is composed of many different shapes, materials, and colors, which cause the building to change color with varying light. Its horizontal elements suggest a pagoda. (Prevalent throughout Asia, a pagoda is a many-storied tower—each story having its own upward-curving roof—usually erected as a temple or monument.) Another important work of this time was the Beth Sholom Temple in suburban Philadelphia. Featuring an unusual pyramidal structure that suggests the tabernacle Moses built for the wandering Israelites, the 250-seat chapel has been called "a mountain of light." Throughout the project, Wright worked closely with Rabbi Mortimer J. Cohen, and, for once, Wright's indisputable stamp seems to have been subordinated to the overall design of a building. He promised the congregation that their temple would be a "Mount Sinai cupped in the hands of God," and, upon viewing, this indeed seems to be a fitting description.

But of all Wright's late work, the most famous is the Solomon R. Guggenheim Museum, which he did not live to complete. Plans for the museum began in the early 1940s, but World War II, Guggenheim's death in 1949, the slow process of buying the property, and much wrangling with the city building authorities held up construction for years. Wright had to agree to many changes imposed by city officials as well as address concerns raised by such painters as Robert Motherwell and Willem de Kooning, who worried that the uneven walls and floors he had designed would do their works an injustice.

After years of delay, construction began in 1957. With its unusual spiral-shaped plan and sloped floors, the building has been compared to the Great White Dagoba, an onion-shaped temple built in Beijing, China, in 1651. In the Guggenheim, Wright most closely united the concepts of form and function. He wanted to display a collection and at the same time suggest the development of a painter or style—to express continuity, change, and totality at once. Wright felt that the ordinary conventions of walls and rooms were antithetical to this aim, so he created a structure in which the viewer, after a short elevator ride, could trace the unfolding of an artist's career while comfortably moving down the spiraling ramps. Because of its unique layout, visitors could also gain perspective on the whole collection by simply turning in to face the center, and they had the option of leaving at any point without retracing their steps.

At the daily afternoon tea, Wright's fellowship apprentices help snap green beans from the Taliesin North garden.

Wright's sketch for the exterior of the Solomon R. Guggenheim Museum in New York City, which opened in the fall of 1959. Because of its curved walls, the building has presented many challenges and problems for the museum's curators, but it remains a masterpiece of modern architecture.

Architectural critics have called the Guggenheim the most sculptural of Wright's creations. There are no posts, beams, confining rooms, or obvious terminal points. Instead, there is only a feeling of continuous movement. Yet the building is also orderly and stable, a monument to the enduring values of art and architecture. Here, as in Falling Water, Wright accomplished the contradictory goals of fluidity and permanence, of stability and change. It may well be one of his finest achievements.

Wright unfortunately did not see the completion of this last great work. Although his health to this point had been excellent, on April 4, 1959, he complained of stomach pains and was taken to a hospital near Phoenix. There he survived an operation for an internal blockage, and his doctors were impressed at how well the 91-year-old came through the surgery. Recovery appeared to be just around the corner. But on April 9, shortly after the attending nurse had checked on him, he breathed a sigh and died.

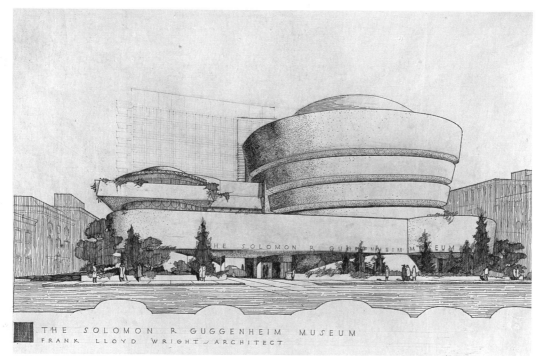

THE SOLOMON R GUGGENHEIM MUSEUM
FRANK LLOYD WRIGHT ARCHITECT

Wright's body was taken back to Spring Green, where a Unitarian funeral service was performed. Attended by about 50 family members, friends, and employees, his coffin was placed on a flower-covered farm wagon and led by a pair of horses to the small family burial ground a few hundred yards from Taliesin. There he was lowered into the ground, not far from where his mother and Mamah Borthwick were buried.

Inside the Guggenheim, a circular ramp coils downward, allowing museumgoers to view the exhibit in a continuous circuit.

All those who had loved and admired him found it hard to believe he was really gone. As a bank cashier in Spring Green said, "He was the kind of man you thought would live forever." Soon after his death, the *Journal of the American Institute of Architects* summed up Wright's contribution to architecture: "His place in history is secure. His continuing influence is assured. This century's architectural achievements would be unthinkable without him. He has been a teacher to us all."

Wright consults with an associate in his studio in 1957. He once observed, "Every great architect is—necessarily—a great poet. He must be a great original interpreter of his time, his day, his age." In a career that spanned more than 70 years, Wright gave shapes and forms to his buildings that were unequaled during his lifetime.

Further Reading

Bolton, Carol R., Robert S. Nelson, and Linda Seidel, eds. *The Nature of Frank Lloyd Wright*. Chicago: University of Chicago Press, 1988.

Farr, Finis. *Frank Lloyd Wright*. New York: Scribners, 1961.

Gill, Brendan. *Many Masks: A Life of Frank Lloyd Wright*. New York: Putnam, 1987.

Kauffman, Edgar, and Ben Raeburn, eds. *Frank Lloyd Wright: Writings and Buildings*. New York: New American Library, 1960.

Pevsner, Nikolaus. *Pioneers of Modern Design*. New York: Penguin Books, 1978.

Pfeiffer, Bruce P., ed. *Frank Lloyd Wright: Letters to Apprentices*. Fresno: California State University Press, 1982.

———. *Frank Lloyd Wright: Letters to Architects*. Fresno: California State University Press, 1984.

Wright, Frank Lloyd. *An Autobiography*. New York: Horizon Press, 1976.

Wright, Olgivanna Lloyd. *Frank Lloyd Wright: His Life, His Work, His Words*. New York: Horizon Press, 1966.

Chronology

June 8, 1867	Born in Richland Center, Wisconsin
1874	Family moves to Weymouth, Massachusetts; mother introduces him to Froebel blocks
1877	Family moves to Madison, Wisconsin
1885	Father abandons family; Wright leaves high school without graduating
1887	Leaves for Chicago; finds employment with Joseph Lyman Silsbee and, some months later, Louis Sullivan
1889	Marries Catherine Tobin
1891	Designs the Charnley house, Chicago, Illinois
1893	Leaves Sullivan's office to establish his own firm
1902	Designs the Willets house, Highland Park, Illinois
1904	Completes Larkin Company Administration Building, Buffalo, New York
1905	Designs Unity Temple, Oak Park, Illinois
1909	Leaves Catherine for Mamah Borthwick, wife of client
1914	Works on Midway Gardens, Chicago, Illinois; tragic fire at Taliesin; death of Borthwick
1915	Wright invites Miriam Noel to live at Taliesin
1916	Begins work on the Imperial Hotel, Tokyo
1920	Completes work on Hollyhock House, Hollywood, California
1923	Completes work on La Miniatura, Pasadena, California; marries Noel
Sept. 1, 1923	Imperial Hotel survives devastating earthquake
1924	Wright meets Olga Milanoff
1927	Divorces Noel
1928	Marries Milanoff

1932	Establishes fellowship at Taliesin
1933	*An Autobiography* is published
1936	Wright designs Falling Water, Connellsville, Pennsylvania
1938	Begins building Taliesin West near Phoenix, Arizona
1939	Completes Johnson Wax Administration Center, Racine, Wisconsin
1943	Conceives early plans for Solomon R. Guggenheim Museum, New York City
1952	Completes Price Tower, Bartlesville, Oklahoma
April 9, 1959	Dies in hospital near Taliesin West

Index

PICTURE CREDITS

Yona Zeldis McDonough received her A.B. from Vassar College and her M.A. from Columbia University. She presently lives in New York City with her husband, photographer Paul McDonough. Her articles and fiction have appeared in many national publications.

Vito Perrone is Director of Teacher Education and Chair of Teaching, Curriculum, and Learning Environments at Harvard University. He has previous experience as a public school teacher, a university professor of history, education, and peace studies (University of North Dakota), and as dean of the New School and the Center for Teaching and Learning (both at the University of North Dakota). Dr. Perrone has written extensively about such issues as educational equity, humanities curriculum, progressive education, and evaluation. His most recent books are: *A Letter to Teachers: Reflections on Schooling and the Art of Teaching*; *Enlarging Student Assessment in Schools*; *Working Papers: Reflections on Teachers, Schools, and Communities*; *Visions of Peace*; and *Johanna Knudsen Miller: A Pioneer Teacher*.

921
Wri   McDonough, Yona
           Frank Lloyd Wright.

U

DEMCO